A People's History of India

Volumes published:

General Editor: Irfan Habib

The Aligarh Historians Society, the sponsor of the project of **A People's History of India**, is dedicated to the cause of promoting the scientific method in history and resisting communal and chauvinistic interpretations.

A PEOPLE'S HISTORY OF INDIA 6

POST-MAURYAN INDIA 200 BC – AD 300

A Political and Economic History

Irfan Habib

Aligarh Historians Society

Tulika Books

Published by
Tulika Books
35 A/1, Shahpur Jat, New Delhi 110 049

First edition (hardback) 2012

Second edition (paperback) 2013

ISBN: 978-93-82381-29-7

Printed at Chaman Enterprises, 1603 Pataudi House,
Daryaganj, Delhi 110 006

Contents

Tables, Maps and Figures

Tables

Maps

Figures

Preface

This volume of the *People's History of India* makes a departure from the preceding two volumes (Nos. 4 and 5) by taking up a very long period (about 500 years), and then dealing with only its political and economic history. This is due to the fact that, partly owing to uncertainties of chronology (especially in the dating of important textual sources as well as political events), there is no apparent line that can be drawn to divide the period. It has therefore become necessary for us to plan two separate monographs (the present No. 6 and the proposed No. 7) to cover different aspects of the history of these five centuries. In monograph No. 7, the social and cultural history of the same period is expected to be covered.

Except for this, I have tried my best to keep in view all the other objectives and features of our series. There are special notes on Numismatics and Elementary Concepts from Economics (now that there is a full chapter on the economy of the period), and on historical problems, viz. the elements of history in the *Purāṇas* and the Shaṅgam (Chankam) texts, and the reconstruction of Kushān chronology. Extracts from sources are appended to each chapter, in the manner that would be familiar to readers of the series.

As in the preceding two monographs, the policy is also followed here of generally reproducing names and terms as they occur in our sources. Thus Prakrit names are not Sanskritized, as is often done by scholars in the interest of uniformity or standardization. Where variant forms are used (mainly in inscriptions and coins), these are usually indicated in this book at first occurrences; minor variations are, however, often ignored.

In this volume we follow a fuller scheme of transliteration of

Sanskrit and Prakrit words, incorporating the partial one adopted in previously published volumes. This is set out below by placing the English letters in the same order as those of the Nagari alphabet:

> a, ā, i, ī, u, ū, ri, rī, ḷ, e, ai, o, au; k, kh, g, gh, ṅ, ch, chh, j, jh, ñ; ṭ, ṭh, ḍ, ḍh, ṇ; t, th, d, dh, n; p, ph, b, bh, m; y, h, l, v, sh, sh, h; ṁ (*anusvāra*), ḥ (*visarga*).

Our Bibliographical notes are principally intended to satisfy the reader's desire for indication of works where further information would be available. These do not, therefore, contain full lists of works that have been used in writing this book.

The note on Elementary Concepts from Economics has had the benefit of a very close scrutiny and much editing from Professor Sayera I. Habib. Faiz Habib has drawn all the maps for this volume, largely based on our joint *Atlas of Ancient Indian History* (New Delhi, 2012), Maps 8 and 9. One exception is this book's Map 4.2(a), which is drawn to scale and scores in accuracy over its source (Inset 1 in Map 8 of the *Atlas*)!

Much gratitude is owed to the libraries of the Department of History, Aligarh, and the Indian Council of Historical Research, New Delhi, and their courteous staff, for making numerous books and journals available to me.

Mr Muneeruddin Khan has patiently processed the entire manuscript. Mr Sajid Islam has carried out the scanning of the illustrations. Mr Arshad Ali has been responsible for much of the paper work that keeps Aligarh Historians Society afloat. Finally, Mr Idris Beg has done most of the inescapable running-about and photocopying required.

Professor Shireen Moosvi, Secretary, Aligarh Historians Society, and Dr Rajendra Prasad and Ms Indira Chandrasekhar of Tulika Books, are, as usual, responsible for getting this book published in time.

IRFAN HABIB

Aligarh
December 2012

1

Greek, Saka (Shaka) and Parthian Dynasties of the North-West and Western India

1.1 Bactrian and Indo-Greek Rulers

Alexander (reigned, 336–323 BC), while conducting his great campaign in Afghanistan, Central Asia and the Indus Basin (331–326 BC), founded a number of settlements in the conquered territories containing both Macedonians (the *elite* group, linguistically distinct from the Greeks) and Greeks, soldiers as well as civilians, to garrison his conquests. After his death, the governors and the garrisons he left behind became involved in the wars among his lieutenants. This gave the Mauryan emperor Chandragupta (322–298 BC) the opportunity to seize a large part of the area in India previously conquered by Alexander. About the year 305 BC, Seleucus, having established himself at Babylon (in Iraq) and Syria, marched eastwards to establish his authority over Bactria (north Afghanistan). Successful in that enterprise, he conceded the region south of the Hindukush to Chandragupta ('Sandracottus'), in order to have peace on his eastern frontier.

It would seem that from this period onwards the Macedonian element began to be gradually absorbed by the larger Greek communities, despite some initial conflicts between the two elements. There was also considerable Greek migration from West Asia. Archaeological remains at Ai Khanum (on the Oxus) and Nimlik, both in Bactria, attest the existence of prosperous Greek settlements: characteristic Greek buildings like the gymnasium and the open theatre have been found at Ai Khanum, along with artefacts made in the true Greek ('Hellenic') tradition. Close connections with the Greek world are attested by the inscription containing Delphic aphorisms set up at Ai Khanum by the philosopher Clearchus in *c.* 275 BC, while he was on his way from Greece to India; and by the translations in impeccable Greek of parts of

Ashoka's Rock Edicts XII and XIII, found inscribed at Qandahar. Ashoka's familiarity with the names of the five major Greek (*Yona*) or Macedonian rulers of the Eastern Mediterranean, mentioned in his Rock Edict XIII, is another remarkable piece of evidence of the close contacts that prevailed between the Greek world and India in the third century BC.

Below the Macedonian and Greek communities in Bactria and Arachosia (Qandahar region) lived the mass of the local population speaking Iranic dialects. Aramaic had been here the language (and script) through which the earlier Iranian or Achaemenid administration had functioned; and it is therefore not surprising that Ashoka's edicts were also rendered into Aramaic at Qandahar and Pul-i Darunta in Afghanistan, as well as at Taxila in north-western Punjab, and at road-stations on the royal highway at Shalatak in Laghman, Afghanistan. At Ai Khanum, a pottery inscription in Aramaic apparently contains an account of tax deliveries from individuals. But Aramaic seems to have fallen out of use in this area by the second century BC, partly perhaps because the local Iranian potentates now took to Greek and its script, as is shown by a Greek inscription at Takht-i Sangin in Bactria set up by an Iranian (Astrosokes) to record a votive present to the Iranian god Vakhshu (river Oxus). Ultimately, in the second century AD, the local people such as were literate would be writing their own East Iranian dialect (now termed Bactrian) in Greek (see *Chapter 3.2*), with systems of transcription suggesting that the shift to Bactrian had begun much earlier, at a time when Greek was still a living language in the area. How upper-class Indian inhabitants of the region could also be similarly Hellenized is illustrated by a long 'funerary' stone inscription composed in Greek by one Sophytos (Subhūtī), *c.* 130 BC, at Qandahar.

After the departure of Seleucus, the Greek settlers south of the Hindukush apparently remained loyal to the Mauryas, while maintaining their autonomous authority in Arachosia, and enjoying a share in the bureaucracy of the empire. A 'Greek official' (*Yavana rāja*), Tushāspha, was Ashoka's governor of Gujarāt, though the name rather suggests that he was a Hellenized Iranian. North of the Hindukush, for the first fifty years of the third century BC, Bactria seems to have remained firmly under the control of the Seleucids; at Ai Khanum in Bactria's eastern corner (modern-day Badakhshan), copper coins of the first three Seleucid rulers, Seleucus (311–281 BC), Antiochus I (281–261 BC) and Antiochus II (261–246 BC), have been found in considerable abundance.

Bactria signalled a crucial political change when, during or immediately after the reign of Antiochus II, the satrapy turned into an independent Greek kingdom. Judging from its archaeological remains, Bactria would seem to have had prosperous cities, though Justin's description of it as possessed of 'a thousand cities' must be deemed gross exaggeration. Its urban prosperity rested apparently on agriculture promoted by irrigation; we have traces of numerous canals in the vicinity of Ai Khanum, quite possibly its first capital.

In time, the governor to whom Bactria was entrusted by the Seleucid court became powerful enough to challenge its authority. Such was Diodotus who, according to Strabo (XI.9.2) and Justin (XLI.4), where the name is misspelt 'Theodotus', declared himself independent around the time (248–247 BC) that Arsaces also raised the banners of revolt in Parthia (south-western Turkmenistan and north-eastern Iran). The separation of Bactria from the Seleucid empire was proclaimed also through their coins by Diodotus I and his son Diodotus II, both of whom issued coins in all the three metals (gold, silver and copper) according to the Attic weight-standard.

The regime of this dynasty must, however, have been of short duration, for when, in *c.* 210–205 BC, Antiochus (III) the Great (223–187 BC) launched his grand campaign to recover the eastern parts of the Seleucid empire, as reported by Polybius (XI.34), it was Euthydemus who was ruling Bactria after having destroyed the descendants of the earlier rebels. Despite a victory in the open field, Antiochus had to leave Bactria without full success. He was able, however, to obtain a number of elephants (then highly prized as war animals in the Hellenistic world) and some tribute from Euthydemus. Antiochus is said to have offered a daughter of his in marriage to Euthydemus's son and successor, Demetrius. Thereafter he crossed the Hindukush to 'renew' the peace with the local Indian ruler Sophagasenus (Subhāgasena), and marched back through Arachosia, which hereafter presumably came under Seleucid rule.

Under Euthydemus the Bactrian Greeks still kept to the north of the Hindukush: his coins bear only Greek legends and conform to the

Attic standard in issues in all the three metals, though possibly a shortage of silver induced him to mint cupro-nickel coins as well. The expansion southward and thence into India began under Demetrius (Strabo, XI.11.1), who was apparently the first ruler to inscribe Kharoshṭhī legends on the reverse of his silver and copper coins minted according to the Indian standard. In Bactria he continued with coins on the Attic standard and with Greek legends alone.

Justin (XLI.6) tells us that one Eucratides seized Bactria from Demetrius about the time that Mithradates I came to the throne in Parthia, an event usually dated *c.* 171 BC. Eucratides's inscription in Greek has been found at Ai Khanum, which has also yielded numerous coins of his. He appears to be the last Bactrian Greek ruler to have coined gold. Like those of Demetrius, many of his coins on the Indian standard have Kharoshṭhī legends, showing that he too had seized some territories within India: the Kharoshṭhī legends on some of his silver coins describe the goddess depicted on the coins' reverse as that 'of the city of Kavishiya', i.e. of Kapisa, Kabul valley. He also overstruck copper coins of Apollodotus I, and so the latter must have preceded him as ruler of some territory. Eucratides's silver coins with paired busts of Heliocles and queen Laodice (*Fig. 1.1.5*) suggest that the pair were his successors, though Heliocles's own coins contain no mention of Laodice as his consort. Justin says that Eucratides was murdered by his son while he was on his way back from his Indian expedition; and Heliocles could have been the son and successor to whom the deed is attributed.

Heliocles had as his contemporaries queen Agathocleia and her son Strato I, some of whose joint coins he restruck. But Strato survived to issue his own coins singly – all bilingual and on the Indian standard, so that he seems to have continued to rule over territory south of the Hindukush. He also restruck some coins of Heliocles.

Such evidence points to the splitting of Greek-ruled territories in Bactria and adjacent areas into separate contending principalities. Along with this division, two simultaneous processes appear to have been set in motion: the loss of Bactria itself to tribes from the north, and the expansion of Greek rule in other parts of Afghanistan and north-western India. In 208–206 BC, in his negotiations with Antiochus III, Euthydemus had emphasized the threat posed by 'huge hordes of nomads' to both Bactria and the Seleucid dominions (Polybius, XI.39). According to Justin (XLI.6), Eucratides had to contend against the Sogdians (across the Oxus), while according to Strabo (XI, 515 and 517), the Parthians to the west of Bactria seized two provinces from Eucratides. The excavators of Ai Khanum have established that this splendid Greek settlement was abandoned by 145 BC, when, it is supposed, it fell into nomads' hands. But 'the Qunduz hoard' (actually found at Khisht-tepe) of Graeco-Bactrian coins, containing Greek legends only and issued by a number of Greek kings including such a late ruler as Hermaeus, suggests that the abandonment of Ai Khanum might have had some other cause and the nomad occupation of Bactria came much later. Strabo (XI.8.2) says, 'the Asioi, the Pasianoi, the Tocharoi and the Sacarauloi [= Sakas; cf. 'Sakai' in Strabo, XI.8.4]' expelled the Greeks from Bactria; but no date is given by him. In view of the Qunduz hoard, that date could be as late as 50 BC (Strabo himself was writing about AD 23).

The second process, viz. intrusion into India, is reported in Indian texts as well as Graeco-Roman sources. The grammarian Patañjali (*c.* 150 BC or later) gives, as an example of a report of current happenings, that of the Yavana besieging Sāketa (Ayodhya) and Madhyamikā (possibly Nagari, near Chittor, Rajasthan). The name of the Greek invader is not supplied. But Strabo (XI.11.1–2) quotes Apollodorus for the statement that the invasions into India were led 'mostly' by Menander but also by Demetrius, son of Euthydemus; and that Menander had crossed the Hypanis (= Hyphasis, the Beas) to reach Imaus (the Yamuna). In addition, both these rulers are said to have subjugated Patalene (Indus delta) and 'the rest of the coast', including the kingdom of Saraostus (Saurashtra) and Sigerdis (?). Given Apollodorus's early date (120 BC), Menander must have reigned around the middle of second century BC, but his exact position in the line of Indo-Greek rulers is not easy to establish. In the famous Buddhist text, the *Milindapañho* ('Questions of Menander'), Milinda or Menander is said to be the Yavana ruler of Shākala or Sialkot. In a casket inscription from Shinkot in Bajaur (North Western Frontier Province NWFP, Pakistan), the local ruler of Apracha (Bajaur) acknowledges the sovereignty of '*maharaja* Minadra'. If at Reh (on the Yamuna, southern Uttar Pradesh), the Brāhmī inscription contains the name 'Mināndra', then, the classical account of Greek occupation of the country along the Yamuna would stand confirmed. As it is, Menander's coins, both of the Attic and Indian standards (the latter bearing Greek and Kharoshṭhī legends), are found in large numbers in Afghanistan and in the Indian plains up to Mathura. The conquest of Saurashtra is, however, doubtful, though it was noted in the *Periplus* of the Erythraean Sea (late first century AD), that the 'ancient drachma' of Apollodotus and Menander were then still current in Barygaza (Bharuch, Gujarāt). But coins could be in use in markets quite outside the dominions of their issuers just because of their good mintage and metal. Incidentally, it is not clear whether the *Periplus* is referring to Apollodotus I or Apollodotus II: the latter's coins are purely of the Indian standard and set a model for the early coinage of the satraps of western India (see *Chapter 1.3*).

There are two other early Indo-Greek rulers, Pantaleon and Agathocles, some of whose coins bear Brāhmī legends, from which one may suppose that they held areas where Brāhmī was in use, i.e. east of the Punjab. Their early date is established from the find of a coin of Agathocles in Ai Khanum (and so of a date before *c.* 145 BC), and from the fact that they imitated Euthydemus in making use of cupra-nickel for their coinage.

A ruler apparently subsequent to Menander was Antialcidas, whose envoy, Heliodorus, has left a Brāhmī inscription at Besnagar (Vidisha, Madhya Pradesh) (see *Extract 1.1*). The inscription says that Heliodorus had come from Takhkhasilā (Taxila), which was presumably Antialcidas's capital, to the court of Bhāgabhadra in the latter's 14th regnal year. If Bhāgabhadra was a late king of the Shunga dynasty, i.e. identical with Bhāgavata of the Purāṇic list and so reigning 115–83 BC (see *Chapter 2.1*), Antialcidas should have reigned around 101 BC.

As the Greek expansion from Bactria to India proceeded apace, the Greek-ruled kingdoms broke into different parts under contending lines. Besides Bactria, Arachosia (Qandahar region), already possessing its own Greek communities, was one such area. Another was the Kabul valley, with Begram as its possible capital. Gandhāra, with capitals at Peucelaotis or Pushkalavati (Charsadda and the neighbouring site of Shaikhan Dheri, NWFP) and Taxila, at both of which 'Greek levels' have been identified by the excavators, could have had at different times its own Greek rulers. The Hathigumpha inscription of Khāravela, the famous ruler of Kalinga during the latter part of the first century BC, seems to mention a Yavana *rāja* of Madhura (Mathura) called Dimita (Demetrius), though this reading is doubtful (see our *Extract 2.2*). There could thus have been a Greek kingdom at Mathura also for some time preceding the Sakas' occupation of Mathura about the time of their emperor Maues's death (*c.* 30 BC) (see *Chapter 1.2* below).

Such multiplicity of Greek-ruled principalities best explains the large number of Graeco-Bactrian and Indo-Greek rulers whose coins have been found – over forty rulers in all for a period of just 200 years. Numismatists have tried to fix sequences, relationships and territorial affiliations by applying a number of criteria, such as divinities portrayed, other symbols used, rulers' portraits and levels of artistry in portraiture, skill in Greek legends, mintage practices, rates of debasement, areas of finds of coins of particular rulers, etc., but little unanimity has yet been attained over many matters, especially in the case of rulers about whom no evidence exists beyond that of their coins.

Among the last Indo-Greek rulers was supposed to be one Hermaeus who issued both Attic standard and Indian standard coins in his own name (he is represented in the Qunduz hoard in Bactria), and also Indian standard coins conjointly with his queen Calliope. His coins have been found over a large area: a thousand of them were recovered from Mir Zakah in Afghanistan. Copper coins were also found containing Hermaeus's bust and name in Greek, and the name of Kajula Kadphises, the first Ku<u>sh</u>ān ruler (*c.* AD 100), in Kharo<u>sh</u>ṭhī, and others where Kajula Kadphises's name appears in Greek (corrupt) and Kharo<u>sh</u>ṭhī but the bust remains that of Hermaeus. It was initially supposed that Hermaeus was kept as the nominal king by the Kushān ruler for some time before being altogether replaced by him. It is, however, now believed that there is no direct transition from Hermaeus's coinage to that of Kajula Kadphises; and that the latter's Hermaeus coins are really imitations, so that there could actually have been a long time-gap between the two rulers. In this case Hermaeus might not have been as late in time (*c.* AD 100) as to have been Kajula Kadphises's contemporary. He probably ruled about 50 BC, by which time Greek hegemony was being brought to an end, both in Bactria and south of the Hindu Kush, by the Sakas and Pahlavas (Parthians) (see *Chapter 1.2* below).

Before leaving the history of Bactrian and Indo-Greek rulers, we may pause to consider what influences on different aspects of life in India, the Greek presence exerted.

The first, most obvious Greek contribution was in the realm of **coinage.** During Mauryan times, and earlier, India knew only of punch-marked coins. Proper coinage in gold, silver and copper, with written 'legends' giving the name of the issuing ruler and the ruler's bust (to catch the attention of the non-literate?), came with the Greek rulers. The Bactrian and Indo-Greek coinage was not a semi-barbarous imitation of Hellenistic models, but is recognized as a notable tradition within Hellenistic coinage. Percy Gardner noted (1886) 'the remarkable originality' of the coiners, recognizing especially 'the extraordinary realism of their portraiture', and he especially singled out the portraits of Demetrius, Antimachus and Eucratides as 'among the most remarkable which have come down to us from antiquity' (see *Figure 1.1*). No subsequent coinage in Ancient India matched the artistic skill of the Greek coinage, though all the subsequent coinage traditions had their ultimate origins in the latter.

Along with coinage, the contacts with the Hellenistic world that the Greeks created led to the introduction of new devices in Indian mechanical arts or **technology.** As we shall see in *Chapter 4.4*, finds at Taxila, datable to the first century AD, include such crucial craft-tools as tongs, pliers, scissors and semi-rotary querns, that had all recently come into use in the Graeco-Roman world.

The excavations at Ai Khanum have re-opened the debate on the extent of Greek influence on Indian **art**. The realism and sureness of touch that could be achieved by Greek artists is represented by the terracotta mould of a veiled woman found there (*Figure 1.2*). Once such artists had arrived in Afghanistan and Taxila, one need not be surprised at the fact that the famous *Yakshi* from Didarganj, Patna, of first century BC, with its Mauryan polish, displays the standard proportions for the torso set in Greek art. The famous Gandhāra art of second century AD, as we shall see, exhibits Graeco-Roman influences, but it is quite probable that the receptiveness to that source of influence was created pre-

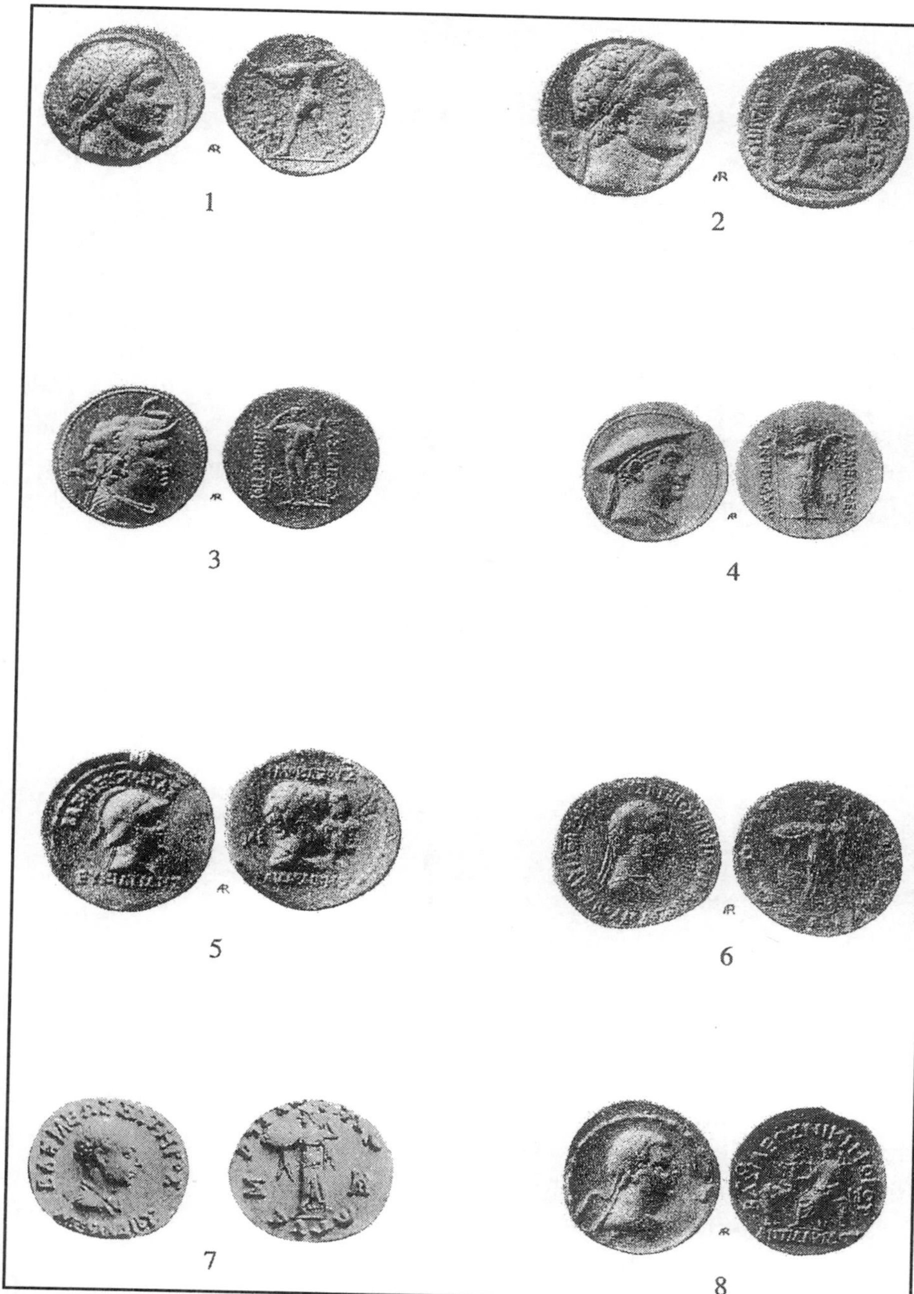

FIGURE 1.1 Silver coins of Greek rulers: (1) Diodotus; (2) Euthydemus; (3) Demetrius; (4) Antimachus; (5) Eucratides, with Heliocles and Laodice; (6) Apollodotus; (7) Menander; (8) Antialcidas.
P. Gardner, except for (7), from R.B. Whitehead.

FIGURE 1.2 Veiled woman, from terracotta mould, Ai Khanum. UNESCO.

cisely because a local Hellenistic tradition already existed in north-western India. One can see this in Kushān coinage, where the Kushāns first imitated the late Greek coinage and then shifted to imitations of Roman gold and copper coins.

Another important area where the Greek presence affected India was the **calendar** and, what was necessarily linked to it, **astronomy**. The initial creation of eras, that is the use of numbered years with the number not remaining confined to a single reign, is attributed to the adoption of the Seleucid era of 312–311 BC by Seleucus I's successors. The early Sakas at Taxila, *c.* 50 BC, were using an era obviously inherited from Greek times, whose epoch lay well beyond 100 BC. Quite telling is the use of Greek or Macedonian months in certain inscriptions, not only in Afghanistan and the Taxila region, but also, as late as the second century AD, at Mathura in Brāhmī (year 28 of the Kushān era). Clearly, with the months must have come the use of Greek calendrical practices by which the solar month was calculated. An actual instance of the passage of Greek astronomy (and astrology) to India is offered by the *Yavana-jātaka* ('Greek horoscope'), composed probably in Prakrit by Yavana-rāja ('Greek master') in Shaka 71 (AD 149) and surviving in its Sanskrit rendering made in Shaka 191 (AD 270) by Sphujidhvaja.

As Greek speakers came to India, some of the words they spoke entered Indian **languages**: in Sanskrit, not only the word *drammaka* for a coin, but also the words for reed-pen (*kalam*), ink (*melā*), horse-bit (*khalīna*, see below under *Chapter 1.3*), tent (*keṇika*), etc., have been borrowed from Greek.

The splendid theatre at Ai Khanum reminds us of the probability that there must have been other places too where Greek communities (and the Hellenized local *elites*) held and watched dramatic performances. Although no direct connection between Greek **drama** and its Sanskrit counterpart can be established, yet from the fact that Sanskrit dramatic compositions begin with Ashvaghosha (second century AD), it can be argued that the observance of theatrical performances in Indo-Greek settlements could have provided the necessary source of stimulus or inspiration for the evolution of drama in Sanskrit.

Finally, **religion**. Down to Mauryan times and later, there is no trace of statuary of gods and goddesses in India. This was in contrast to the Greek practice where the divinities had definite human forms, postures and appendages. They (Zeus, Heracles, Apollo, Poseidon) appear on Graeco-Bactrian and Indo-Greek coins, notably those which conform to the Attic standard. On those coins of Pantaleon and Agathocles which bear a Brāhmī legend, a goddess appears on the obverse that has been likened to an 'Indian dancing girl'. Since these two rulers belonged to about the middle of the second century BC, this could be a very early attempt to portray a goddess like Pārvati. Indian deities actually appear on Parthian but especially Kushān coins, seemingly to replace Greek deities on the reverse. By Kushān times (second century

MAP 1.1 The North-West under Greeks, Sakas and Parthians

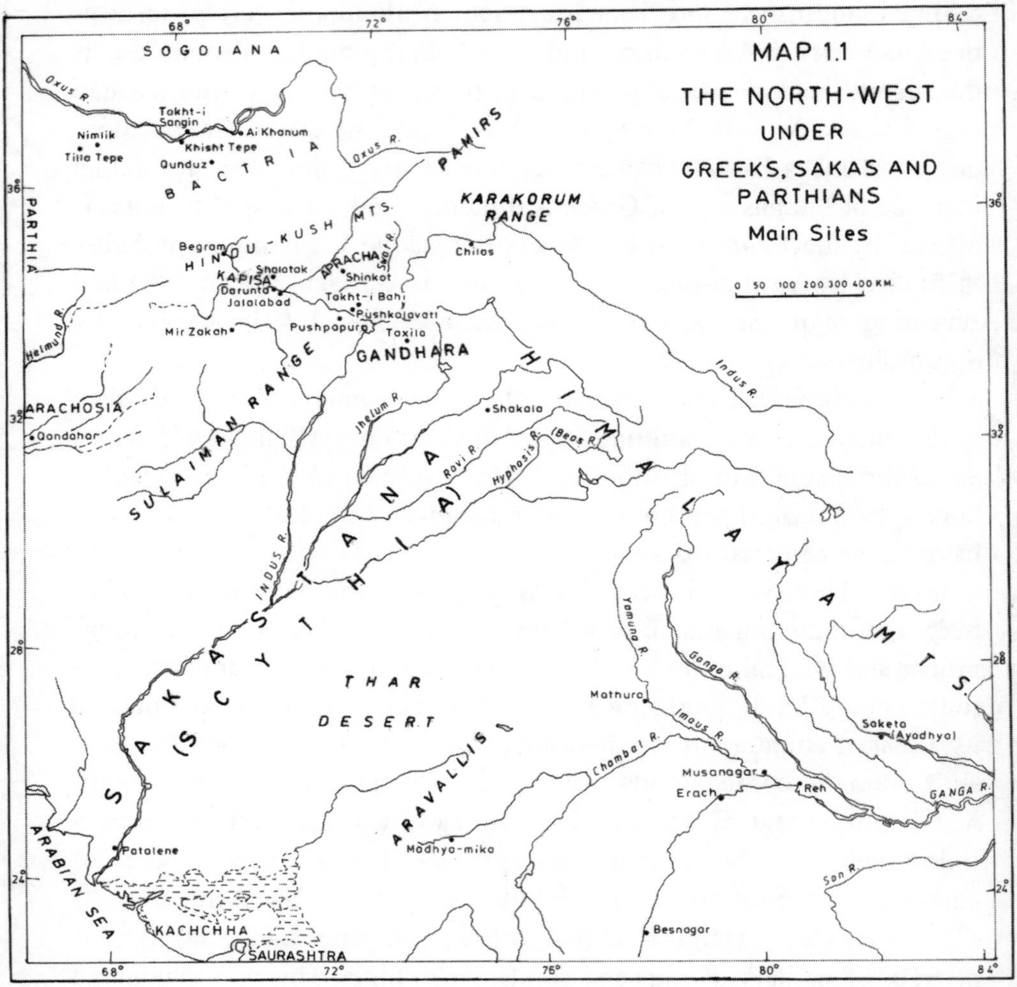

AD), the basic canons of Indian iconography, at least in relation to the Buddha and the god Shiva, appear to have been established. An indirect Greek source of inspiration behind the emergence of Indian iconography cannot, therefore, be ruled out.

1.2 The Early Sakas (Shakas) and Pahlavas

The Sakas or Shakas, unlike the Yonas and Kāmbojas (people of Kabul valley), are not mentioned in any Indian text or inscription before the end of Mauryan times. But they were known to the Achaemenids of Iran who, in their inscriptions, distinguished between three sets of Sakas, one of them being described as Sakā Tigraxauda (or Sakas with pointed caps), who are shown on Persepolis reliefs (fifth century BC) as bearing tribute, accompanied by a horse. Apparently, they were horse breeders of the Central Asian steppes. Herodotus speaks of the Sacae (distinct from the Scythians on the Black Sea coast) who formed a part of the Achaemenid army. After Alexander crossed the Oxus in 330–329 BC, the Sakas inhabiting Trans-oxiana rose in revolt and raided Bactria. Alexander suppressed or conciliated his opponents at that time, but it is likely that the nomads, of whom Euthydemus is reported to have complained to Antiochus III in 208–05 BC, were Sakas. Chinese sources suggest that some time after 200 BC, the Sai or Sak people, who inhabited lands up to northern Xinjiang (West China), came under pressure from the Yueh-chi, themselves driven westwards by the Hiung–nu (the Huns?). According to Strabo, Greek rule in Bactria was overthrown by the Sakas and some other tribes; and we have suggested that this event probably came about as late as 50 BC. There is, however, no evidence – numismatic or other – which yields us the name of any Saka ruler of Bactria.

The first Saka king who enters known history is Maues, whose coins are found mainly in the Punjab but not in Afghanistan. The coins bear his name, in Greek: Mauou, in Kharoṣhṭhī: Moa (*Figure 1.3*). The Greek letters on his coins are still written in the round and so his date has been held to be earlier than the 20s BC; indeed his coins (*Figure 1.*3) are said to be of better quality than those of Hermaeus, the Greek ruler whom we have encountered above. His use of the Greek title *Basileus Basileon*, 'King of Kings', rendered as *rajatiraja* in Kharoṣhṭhī, was borrowed from the Parthian emperors, and represents a new claim to imperial dignity; it also suggests a date somewhere about mid-first century BC for his reign.

Numismatic evidence, combined with what the inscriptions divulge to us, enable us to reconstruct the history of the Saka and Pahlava rulers from Maues onward, with some success achieved in establishing relative chronology, though any degree of exactitude in absolute chronology (in dates BC/AD) still eludes us. First of all, we learn from a copper-plate inscription from Taxila, of year 78 of an unknown era, that in the town of Takhashila (Taxila) there then ruled Liaka Kusulaka, of the Kshaharata clan, the *kshatrapa* of Chukhsa district, along with his son Patika, under the *maharaya* (great king), the great Moga. In the far north, near Chilas, on the modern Karakorum highway, there is an inscription of Sidhalaka, *kshatrapa* of the great (*mahataka*) Moga. In Moga we can recognize emperor Moa (Maues) of the coins. Some time later, at Mathura was inscribed in Kharoshṭhī a long inscription on a stone lion-capital (*Extract 1.2*), which refers to 'Kusula Patika, the *mahakshatava*', obviously the Patika of the Taxila copper-plate who had now become the holder of a title still higher than that of his father. Secondly, it states that the 'shri-raya' (*shrī-rāja*), the illustrious king Muki, was dead, and funeral solemnities were being held for him and his horse. King Muki, held to be identical with Moga of the Taxila copper-plate, must therefore be Maues. Finally, the entire *entourage* of the dead king is shown as being involved in making a grant of land to a Buddhist monastery at Mathura, to secure honour, among others, for 'Sakastana', or the Saka dominion or homeland, its name displaying a very early use of the Iranian territorial suffix, -*stān*. Wherever 'Sakastana', in the eyes of Maues's *entourage*, was situated (see below), the reference establishes clearly that Maues himself and members of his nobility were Sakas.

It is possible that the lion-capital inscription was set up after Maues had been driven out from Taxila. An inscription, dated year 81, has been found at Jalalabad in lower Kabul valley in Afghanistan, which refers to Tīravharana as the *kshatrapa* of Pushpapura, but makes no reference to the paramount sovereign, so that the emperor Moga (Maues), mentioned in Liaka Kusulaka's Taxila inscription dated three years earlier, was probably no longer on the scene. Apollodotus II, who overstruck Maues's coins, could possibly have gained from Maues's exit, though some of his own coins were counterstruck by Maues, so that a conflict with varying fortunes is possible.

The lion-capital inscription's list of members of Maues's *entourage*, all apparently present at Mathura at the time, is most interesting. The inscription was set up at the direction of Ayasia Kamuia, the daughter of the crown-prince Kharaosta and wife of *mahākshatrava* Rajula (Rajuvula), whose son, *kshatrava* Shuḍasa, made the actual grant. Besides giving the names of numerous family members, female and male, the inscription goes on to mention *mahākshatava* Patika, *kshatrava* Mevaki Miyika and Khardaa, *kshatrava* of 'Takshila' (Taxila). The Kharoshṭhī characters in which the inscription is written signify immediately that Maues's *entourage* had come from the north-west, with their scribes knowing only Kharoshṭhī, the script in use at Taxila, and not Brāhmī, which was in use at Mathura. The mention of Taxila shows that the town was still claimed for Maues. As to Sakastana: it could have been modern Seistan, for the name 'Sakastane Sakōn Skythōn' was applied to that region (or rather, a region lying between Zarangeane and Arachosia) by Isidorus in his *Mansiones Parthicae.* It could also have meant the Scythia of *Periplus* or Sind adjacent to Kachchh.

The Saka empire itself was already on the eve of breaking up. Kharaosta, the 'crown-prince' in the Mathura lion-capital inscription, has left behind copper coins with Greek and Kharoshṭhī legends in which he claims to be no more than a satrap (*kshatrapa*). Rajuvula, described as *mahakshatrava* in the lion-capital inscription, also issued coins as an independent sovereign, with corrupt Greek and Kharoshṭhī legends, only as a satrap (*kshatrapa*). But his coins with Greek and Brāhmī legends represent him as a *mahākhatapa*; and he is designated *mahākshatrapa* also in the Mora well inscription near Mathura, which is one of the earliest extant Sanskrit inscriptions in India. His son, Shoḍāsa, is mentioned as a reigning *mahākshatrapa* in a number of inscriptions (all in Brāhmī) found in Mathura and its vicinity. One of these inscriptions bears the year 72, which cannot, however, be of the same era as the earlier Taxila copper-plate of year 78. Shoḍāsa's coins are fewer than those of his father and found over a much smaller area within western Uttar Pradesh.

It is indeed likely that Mathura was the last stronghold of a rapidly fragmenting and territorially contracting Saka empire. This

FIGURE 1.3 Coins of Maues: (1) Silver; (2) Copper, Attic standard; (3) Copper, Indian style. R.B. Whitehead.

apparently transitional polity, however, contained some features which are worth noting. Obviously, it inherited a Greek-knowing establishment, whose influence decayed as the Saka centre moved from Taxila to Mathura. Its high nobility consisted of dynastic governors, styled 'satraps'/*kshatrapas*, a title from old Iranian *kshatra-pāvan*, 'lord (*pāvan*) or protector of a province (*kshatra*)'. Once a *kshatrapa* became more powerful or independent, the Indian term *mahā-*, 'great', was prefixed to his title.

Culturally, the Sakas appear to have introduced a new foreign element, namely, their Iranian dialect. Most early Saka names, as for example in the Mathura lion-capital inscription, were Iranian in origin. The Sakas must have used Iranian words in administration as well, as is illustrated by the designation of a treasurer in an inscription at Mathura of the time of *mahākshatrapa* Shoḍāsa, viz. *gaṁjavara*, the same as Persian *ganj-var*, treasure-keeper. Maues's coins contain representations exclusively of Greek deities, though his great chiefs at Mathura came together to make a donation of land as *dhamadana* (*dharma-dāna*) to a Buddhist monastery, to record which they set up the Mathura lion-capital inscription. But the Sakas must have continued with their own customs and beliefs as well: the same Mathura lion-capital inscription shows that in the Saka funeral rites, the dead master's horse was a part of the ceremony, probably slaughtered to accompany its master, an archaeologically attested Central Asian custom.

The break-up of Maues's empire opened the doors for a **Parthian (Pahlava)** incursion. Their story seems to begin with Vonones (a name shared with two kings of the imperial Parthian line), whose silver and copper coins are found mainly in southern Afghanistan. He is likely to have been the ruler of Seistan and Arachosia (Qandahar region). His name, with full titles, appears in Greek on the obverse of his coins, but in the Kharoshṭhī legends the same titles are given to his 'brother' Spalahores and then to the latter's 'son' (so described on the coins), Spalagadames. On his own coins Spalahores came to be represented as Spalyris or Spalirises (whence Kharoshṭhī: Shpalirisha). On some of his coins the name of Spalgadames, his son, appears in Kharoshṭhī on the reverse, and in some others Azes ('Aya'). Since all those mentioned in the Kharoshṭhī legends of the coins of Vonones and Spalirises are also given royal titles, one must assume that the closest member of the royal family (possibly the recognized heir) was given the right to govern the area where Kharoshṭhī was in use, i.e. Arachosia, while the senior sovereign ruled over Seistan.

It was apparently Azes (I) who moved from Arachosia to Gandhara to supplant the early Sakas (or, alternatively, Apollodotus II). Even after distinguishing Azes I's coinage from that of Azes II, its size remains impressive. Changes made in forms of Greek lettering make Azes I's coins subsequent to those of Maues, and suggest a date for him within the range of 30 BC – AD 8. This excludes the possibility suggested by J. Marshall, and now by G. Fussman and others, that Azes I's accession took place in 57 BC, and that the era he founded was the Vikrama era. Though we must deny him this honour, he has still a claim to immortality because he is the first historical ruler in India to establish an era that came to be named after him. The era of *mahārāya* Aya or Aja, i.e. Azes, is expressly used to date some inscriptions from NWFP (years 63, 74, 126, 134) and one from Taxila (year 136). The continuous use of the era in this area indicates that it formed his core territory, as is indeed confirmed by the find-spots of most of his coins.

These dated inscriptions, with the aid of coins, help to establish the relative chronology of the rulers of the dynasty. In line with the practice of this Parthian dynasty, Azes I began to have on the reverse of his coins the name and full titles of Azilises ('Ayilisha' in the Kharoshṭhī legend) (*Figure 1.4:1*). Azilises succeeded Azes I to mint coins solely in his own name; but one silver coin of his has the name of Azes (II) in Kharoshṭhi on the reverse. Azes II's coins show increasing debasement of both the Greek script and the silver employed. On some copper coins of Azes II, the Kharoshṭhī legend on the reverse enters the name of Indravarma's son Aspavarma, the *strategos* (Greek word in the Prakrit form *stratega*, meaning subordinate ruler) (*Figure 1.4:2*). Indravarma himself is the author of an inscription from the Swat valley, dated in the year 63 of 'the Great King Aya, deceased', wherein he is called the ruler of Apacha (Bajaur, NWFP). Aspavarma, again described as a *strategos* and the son of Indravarma, appears also on the reverse of some copper coins of Gondophares in the Kharoshṭhī legend (*Figure 1.4:3*). These facts show that Aspavarma first served Azes II, some time after the year 63 of Azes I's accession, and then similarly served Gondophares, who must therefore have succeeded Azes II.

Figure 1.4 **(1) Silver coin of Azes I and Azilises; (2) Copper coin of Azes II with *strategos* Aspavarma; (3) Copper coin of Gondophares with *strategos* Aspavarma**

This enables us immediately to infer that in the Takht-i Bahi (NWFP) inscription of Gondophares (also spelt Gondopharnes), the date – year 103 – is to be assigned to the Azes era, and since the inscription also gives year 26 as (presumably) Gondophares's regnal year, he must have ascended the throne in year 77 of the Azes era. Since the Azes era probably began during 30 BC – AD 8, Gondophares's reign must be taken to have begun between AD 47 and 85 and to have lasted for over twenty-six years. It is of some interest to note that Gondophares appears in third-century Christian legend as the Indian ruler to whose court St Thomas went after Christ's Crucifixion in AD 39. The historical value of the legend is small, but it may still indicate very roughly the period (with a large margin of error!) when Gondophares ruled. The territory that Gondophares ruled over besides Taxila and NWFP, in which his Takht-i Bahi inscription is located, cannot be established with certainty. If he is the 'Gendavahara *raja*' in a rock inscription near Chilas on the Karakorum highway, his dominions could have extended up the Indus valley to the feet of the Karakorum range. But how far his writ extended over southern Punjab or Sind, we have no means of knowing.

Gondophares appears to have had two (rival?) successors, both of whom used royal titles and his name: Abdagases as 'brother's son of Gondophares', and Orthagnes as his kinsman. The *Periplus* of Erythraean Sea, which was compiled in the late first century AD, seems to describe the situation that had now emerged. It (Sections 37–38) calls the region of the Indus plains down to the Indus delta by the name of Scythia (compare 'Sakastana' of the Mathura lion-capital inscription), and its capital in the interior 'Minnagara' (not identified). It was governed, it says, 'by Parthian princes, who are perpetually at strife among themselves, especially each the other'. Among such princes is probably to be placed a ruler called *kshatrapa* Jihunia, son of *kshatrapa* Manigula, on his coins (Greek form of name: Zeionises). He is mentioned in the Taxila silver-vase inscription of the year 191 as an unnamed *maharaja*'s brother, with his own name spelt as Jihoṇika, the *kshatrapa* of Chakhsa, a locality near Taxila. If the year refers to the same era in which the earlier *kshatrapa* of Chukhsa, Liaka Kusulaka's Taxila inscription of year 78 of Maues's time is dated, Jihoṇika should have been ruling during Gondophares's reign or a little later. That he could issue coins of his own with no reference on them to the *maharaja* mentioned in his inscription, shows how much the Parthian regime had weakened at this time.

Indeed we can, at least in terms of the Azes era, fix the time by which the Parthians had lost Taxila. Expressly recording its date of year 136 in the 'Aya' era, the Taxila silver-scroll inscription acknowledges the sovereignty of a Kushān ('Khushaṇa') emperor (name not given). Dated not expressly in the Azes era but presumably using the same era, the Panjtar inscription on the Indus north of Taxila bears the year 122 and refers to the reign of *maharaya* (emperor) Gushana. This means that within nineteen years of the Takht-i Bahi inscription of Gondophares (itself datable to some time after AD 73), the Kushāns from Bactria had taken over possession of the Indo-Parthians' core territory of Taxila and surrounding region.

Of the cultural affinities of the Parthians during their century of rule from Azes onwards, little is known. On their coins they continued to depict Greek deities, notably Zeus and Pallas, and, less importantly, Nike and Heracles. But under Azilises, the goddess Lakshmī also appears on the reverse of his coins; and Gondophares extends recognition to god Shiva, who carries his trident on his coins.

From the Parthian-ruled territories there could also have been some Parthian migration into further India. As we shall just see, the coins of Chashṭana of Gujarat and Nahapāna in northern Maharashtra suggest affinities with the Parthian regime in the Indus basin. This is reinforced by the mention of a 'Pahlava' (Parthian), Suvishākha, son of Kulaipa, as minister and governor of Anarta and Surāshṭra under the Gujarāt Shaka ruler Rudradāman, in the Junagadh rock inscription of AD 150.

1.3 The Shaka (Saka) Rulers of Gujarāt and Mahārāshṭra

The history of the so-called 'Western Satraps' or Shaka rulers of Gujarāt comes as a relief to the historian for here, at least, he gets a firm chronological framework, based on the Shaka era of AD 78 in which the rulers' inscriptions and coins are dated (the latter from year 102 of that era onwards). The earliest indication of Shaka power in Gujarāt is provided by the finds of a few copper coins issued by two *kshatrapas*, viz. 'Kshaharata' Agudaka, whose coins found in Kachchh only bear Greek and Brāhmī legends, and Bhūmaka, also a Kshaharata, with coins bearing Greek, Kharoshṭhī and Brāhmī legends, found over a larger area of western India. The Greek and Kharoshṭhī characters suggest connection with the Indus basin. This association is emphasized by the large number of coins of *rājño* (king) *mahākshatrapa* **Chashṭana**, son of Ghsamotika (Syamotika), carrying Prakrit in Greek, Kharoshṭhī and Brāhmī legends, found in Gujarāt. We have also coins of *rajño* 'Ksharata' **Nahapāna** with legends in all the three scripts as on Chashṭana's coins, but found in much larger numbers (*Figure 1.5:1*): over 13,000 silver issues by him have been found in a hoard near Nasik (northern Maharashtra) and in a small hoard at the Saurashtra port of Ghogha. Chashṭana's and Nahapāna's coins are so very similar, with three scripts being used in the same fashion, that it may be presumed that they were contemporaries and that their power had originated in the same polity in the Indus basin, possibly in the Parthian kingdom of Gondophares. Chashṭana's inscription from Daulatpur (Kachchh) is dated his 6th 'regnal year' and other inscriptions, all from Andhau (Kachchh), are dated years 11 and 52 (= AD 89 and 130). Those of the reign of Nahapāna at Nasik and Junnnar mention years 41, 42, 45 and 46, which would correspond to AD 119, 120, 123 and 124, if they are of the Shaka era. But given the likelihood that the Shaka era began with Chashṭana's accession, there seems little reason for Nahapāna to have used that era. The *Periplus* of the Erythraean Sea (Section 41), which cannot be assigned to any time later than AD 106, reports that 'Barygaza' (Bharuch), then an important port, was ruled over by 'Manbanus', a name emended to 'Nambanus' and then identified with Nahapāna. If this emendation is accepted, Nahapāna must have been in occupation of Bharuch well before AD 106; and his inscriptions could then be using an era whose epoch lay about AD 50.

Nahapāna had a powerful son-in-law, Ushavadāta, who, in one of his Nasik and Karle cave inscriptions, describes himself as a 'Shaka'. Ushavadāta's Nasik inscriptions record generous grants made to Brahmans at a number of places, which suggest that Nahapāna's territories extended from Soparaga (Sopara near Mumbai) to Ujeni (Ujjain, Madhya Pradesh), Dashapura (Mandsaur) and even possibly Pokshara (Pushkar near Ajmer), and included Bharukachchha (Bharuch) and Prabhasa (Somnath) in Gujarat. Nasik was probably his capital. In Nahapāna's last inscription at Junnar, south of Nasik, of the year 46 (= *c.* AD 96?), his designation is raised from *kshatrapa* to *mahā-kshatrapa*.

Nahapāna's power seems to have come to an end shortly afterwards. Over 9,000 of his 13,000 silver coins in the Nasik hoard are counterstruck by Gotamīputa Sātakaṇi, the Sātavāhana ruler. At Nasik Gotamīputa has actually left an inscription, dated his 18th regnal year, in which he disposes of land previously held by Ushavadāta ('Usabha-data'); and his successor Vāsiṭhīputa Pulumāyi, in his Nasik inscription of his 19th regnal year (*Extract 2.3*), attributes to Gotamīputa the destruction of 'the Khaharata race' (the clan of Nahapāna) and conquest of territories which had at least in part been under Nahapāna's control, such as Suraṭha (Saurashtra), Aparanta (Konkan) and Ākara-Avati (Avanti, Malwa).

The overthrow of Nahapāna's power seems to have also opened the way for Chashṭana to claim a share out of his dominions. This possibly led him to a conflict with Gotamīputa Sātakaṇi, for it is claimed for the latter that besides destroying the Khaharata race, he also worsted in battle 'Sakas, Yavanas and Palhavas', a motley enemy by which Chashṭana's forces are likely to be meant. In his inscription at Andhau of year 11 (AD 89) Chashṭana is only a *kshatrapa*, and in those of year 52 (AD 130) at the same place, just a *rāña*, sharing sovereignty with his grandson Rudradāman; but in his coins his designation is altered to *mahākshatrapa*. Ptolemy, who wrote between AD 146 and *c.* 170, while giving an account of India, describes 'Ozene' (Ujjain) as 'the capital of Tiastenes', a ruler usually identified with Chashṭana, whose name in Greek letters on his coins is in fact spelt 'Tastansa'.

In the famous Junagadh rock inscription (in Sanskrit) of Chashṭana's grandson and successor **Rudradāman**, set up some time after the year 72 (= AD 150), the territories the latter claims to possess include Akara-Avanti (Malwa), Surāshṭra and Aparānta (all three of which had been claimed on behalf of Nahapāna and, then, of Gotamīputa Sātakarṇi). Rudradāman also held Sindhu-Sauvira (Sind), through which the Western Satraps might well have originally entered Gujarat. He claims to have twice defeated Sātakarṇi, who is probably to be identified with Vasishṭhīputra Sātakarṇi. It is obvious that despite the claims made by Rudradāman, Aparānta remained outside the limits of

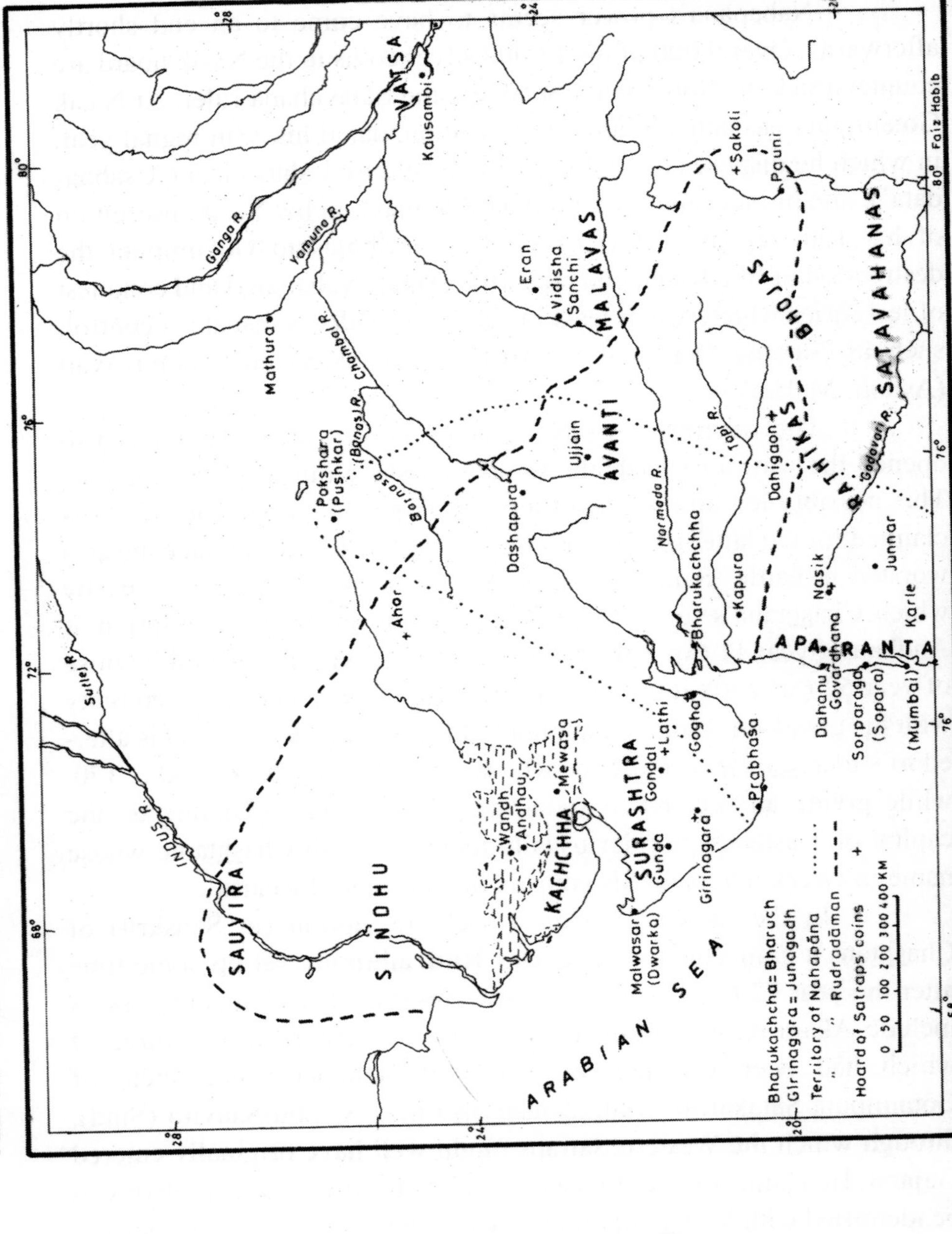

Map 1.2 Western India under the Satraps

his control, since a series of Sātavāhana inscriptions are found at not only Nasik, but also at Kanheri and Karle caves – and none of Rudradāman or his line.

Like Cha<u>sh</u>ṭana, Rudradāman appears on his coins as *mahāk<u>sh</u>atrapa*; he does us some service by stating in his Junagadh inscription that this title was self-assumed, that is, not granted by anyone. Despite the earlier sense of satrap or *k<u>sh</u>atrapa* as a governor, by this time it meant a king, while *mahāk<u>sh</u>atrapa* tended to be a higher title denoting a paramount ruler. Among the Western Satraps, as we can see from their inscriptions and coins, the principal ruler was called *mahāk<u>sh</u>atrapa* and the designated heir, often a brother or nephew, was designated *k<u>sh</u>atrapa*, though sometimes on coins the title *k<u>sh</u>atrapa* might also appear instead of *mahāk<u>sh</u>atrapa* for the principal ruler as well. There is no basis for assuming that when Cha<u>sh</u>ṭana had claimed to be a *k<u>sh</u>atrapa* only, he acknowledged subordination to a superior power, whether Parthian or Kushān.

The Satraps' silver coinage is of great interest. From the year 102 (AD 180), the coins began to carry the date (in Shaka years) of mintage on the obverse, an important innovation, which enables us to reconstruct much of the Satraps' dynastic history (*Fig. 1.5:2*). Hoards of the Satraps' silver coins have been found in Saurashtra, Marwar, upper Mahi valley, near Sanchi, in middle Tapti valley and beyond the Wainganga river, suggesting a fairly large territory where their coins were current. A large hoard found south of the Krishna river in coastal Andhra, however, shows that their coins were in use even where the Satraps' writ as rulers could not possibly have run. The Satraps' own inscriptions are confined to Kachchh and Saurashtra, except one doubtfully ascribable to Rudrasena I of year 127 (AD 205), found at Devni-Mori (north-eastern Gujarāt), and another in memory of a *mahākhattava-kumāra* at Pauni on the Wainganga. From a coin of one Īshvaradatta Ābhīra (year 154 = AD 232), claiming to be a *mahāk<u>sh</u>atrapa,* it is possible to infer some disturbance at the time in the political structure of the Shaka kingdom. The fabric and quality of the silver coins begin to show signs of degradation from the later issues of Vijayasena, *c.* year 167 (AD 245); and it may be supposed that a contraction in resources and, therefore, possibly of the dominions of the Satraps might have set in from about that time.

FIGURE 1.5 Silver coins of (1) Nahapāna and (2) Dāmasena, of year 153 (AD 233). C.J. Brown.

The Shaka kingdom probably suffered a reduction in its territory to the east owing to the expansion of the Kushān empire. The Kushān emperor Kaṇi<u>sh</u>ka, in his Rabatak inscription (*c.* AD 160), claims possession of 'Ozene' (Ujjain), and two Kushān inscriptions at Sanchi (*c.* AD 182 and 188) establish the fact of Kushān control over that part of central India. Upon the decline of the Kushān empire, a Shaka chief, Shrīdharavarman, established his authority in this area. In an inscription near Vidisha of (Shaka) year 201 (AD 279), corresponding to his regnal year 13, he designates himself a *mahādaṇḍanāyaka*, a Kushān title; but at Eran nearby, in another inscription of his, of regnal year 27 (AD 293), he calls himself a *mahāk<u>sh</u>atrapa*. The Western Satraps themselves probably never regained suzerainty over Malwa.

On the plane of titular claims, the Western Satraps appear to have received some setback after Shaka year 221 (AD 299), when the reign of Bhart<u>ri</u>dāman as *mahāk<u>sh</u>atrapa* ended. His successors remained mere *k<u>sh</u>atrapas* till the year 254 (AD 332). Then, after a hiatus, the title of *mahāk<u>sh</u>atrapa* was revived by Svāmi Rudrasena, and maintained from year 270 (AD 348) onwards. All the *mahāk<u>sh</u>atrapas* now bore the title *svāmi*. The coins of the last of them (Rudrasiṁha) carry the years 309 to 337 (AD 387–415). His last years were probably involved in a struggle with the Guptas: Chandragupta II (d. 414–15) began to issue coins in silver on the model of the Satraps' issues, one of which is dated (Gupta) year 90 or 90+ (AD 410+), proclaiming in effect the Gupta annexation of the Satrapal kingdom.

The social and cultural impact of the Shaka power, maintained for some three centuries in western India, calls for a few reflections. There was undoubtedly some immigration from the north-west. In a Nasik cave inscription there is record of a cave created for Buddhist monks by a Yona (Greek) bearing an Indian name, but described as 'a northerner' from Dattāmitrī, the name of a city called Demetrius after the Greek ruler of that name in Arachosia. Nahapāna, the Shaka prince to whose time this inscription could belong, was, like Cha<u>sh</u>ṭana, still using Greek characters on his coins, though these were used now to transcribe a Prakrit legend rather than any phrase in Greek. Probably, knowledge of the Greek language was already lost at these princes' courts. Rudradāman's minister, who rebuilt the Sudarshana lake at Girnar near Junagadh, was, as we have seen, a Pahlava or Parthian, who, like the Shakas, spoke an Iranian dialect. The names of Cha<u>sh</u>ṭana and Nahapāna were Iranic, and so also the name of Rudradāman I's successor Dāma-ghsada, where *-ghsada* (later form, *-jada*) is held to represent the Persian word *-zāda*, '[well-]born'. In a later Nasik cave inscription, a well-placed Shaka woman gave a large donation of money ('1000 *kar<u>sh</u>āpaṇa*') for the relief of sick Buddhist monks; and there are also two records of donation made by a Shaka from Dashapura (Mandsor). The adoption of Indian names by rulers of Cha<u>sh</u>ṭana's line was not the only sign of the assimilation of these immigrants into Indian society. Rudradāman's Junagadh rock inscription (*Extract 1.3*) is regarded as the first inscription to carry a text in pure classical Sanskrit. That ruler was already conscious of caste divisions, as he proclaims for himself the allegiance of all the *varnas.* While taking pride in defeating the Yaudheyas, who had gloried in 'their title of heroes among the K<u>sh</u>atriyas', he or his draftsman does not omit to assert his respect for cows and Brāhmaṇas.

The Junagadh rock inscription is also important because it casts some light on the mode of **finance** of the government. The three sources for filling the treasury are said to be *bali*, *shulka* and *bhāga.* The first and the third make us recall the imposts mentioned in Ashoka's Rummeindi pillar inscription: the village of Luṁmini was exempted from *bali* (*ubalike*) and the tax on crops was reduced to *aṭha-bhāga*, one-eighth of the produce. One assumes, then, that *bali* was a general levy imposed on the whole village, while *bhāga* represented the share of produce separately taken as tax. *Shulka* appears in the *Arthashāstra* (2.22.2) as toll or duty. The size of taxation so extracted must have been considerable, because Rudradāman declares that his treasury was overflowing with treasure. The same inscription also reminds us of three other oppressive burdens that the state lay upon the people (*jana*) of town and country (*paurajānapada*): tax (*kara*), forced labour (*vishṭi*), and arbitrary 'benevolences' or exactions (*praṇaya-kriya)*. Though these may not have been resorted to for rebuilding the Sudarshana lake, as is claimed in the inscription, they were clearly sources on which the state could draw in addition to its usual tax levies. What the Western Satraps attained by their stable silver currency in its pre-debasement stage, i.e. at least till about *c*. AD 245, was the creation of an efficient medium through which taxes could be collected from their subjects.

The other important part of government was represented by the **army**. Here, as with the early Sakas, cavalry seems to have enjoyed a favoured role. The Saka emperor Maues put the image of a horseman with a spear on his coins; and the Mathura lion-capital inscription makes a specific reference to his horse. In the Junagadh rock inscription Rudradāman is commended for his management of 'horses, elephants and chariots' – in that order. Much advantage always lay with invaders from the north-west owing to their access to good war-horses, which, because of climate, could not be bred well in India. Another matter to be considered here is the further advantage obtained by the Greeks, Parthians and Shakas, in that while they could control their horses by use of horse-bits, their Indian opponents had to manage with the far less efficient nose-bands, as shown in Sanchi sculpture (*Figure 1.6*; see also *Figure 4.6* for nose-straps depicted in a Mathura panel). (When the Greek sources say that Indians did not use the bridle, they presumably mean the horse-bit, rather than the horse's head-gear.) Until the Indians too learnt to use horse-bits, with the Greek word for it getting the Sanskrit form *khalīna,* the advantage to their opponents in the battle-field could have been decisive.

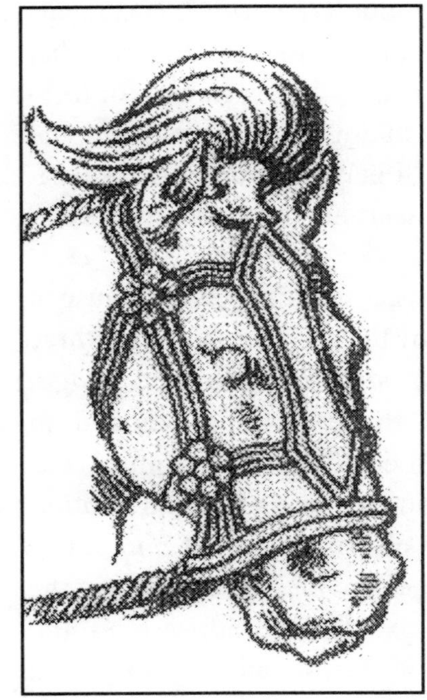

FIGURE 1.6 Horse with nose-band (in lieu of horse-bit), west gateway, Sanchi. F.C. Maisey.

TABLE 1.1 Chronology

	BC
Alexander's campaign in Afghanistan, Central Asia and Indus basin	331–326
Ai Khanum founded on the Oxus under Seleucids	*c.* 300
Bactria independent, under Diodotus I	*c.* 248–247
Antiochus the Great's campaign against Bactria	208–205
Eucratides becomes ruler of Bactria	*c.* 171
Menander, conqueror of large territories in India	*c.* 150
Besnagar inscription of the envoy of Antialcidas, of Taxila	*c.* 101
Greek rule overthrown in Bactria	*c.* 50
Saka (Shaka) emperor Maues ruling at Taxila	*c.* 50
Azes I, accession at Taxila; establishes era	30 BC – AD 8
	AD
Gondophares, accession	post-47
Shaka era established	78
Nahapāna, *kshatrapa/mahākshatrapa*, at Nasik	*c.* 90
Chashṭana, *kshatrapa/mahākshatrapa*, in Gujarāt	78–130
Rudradāman I's Junagadh rock inscription	150
The *svāmi-mahākshatrapas* of Gujarat	348–415
Fall of the Western Satraps; Gupta annexation	414

Extract 1.1

The Besnagar (Vidisha) Inscription of Heliodorus, *c.* 120 BC (Prakrit in Brāhmī characters)

Of the god of gods, Vāsudeva, this Garuḍa flag-staff was erected by Heliodora [Heliodorus], his (the god's) devotee (*bhāgavata*), the son of Diya [Dion], from Takhkhasilā [Taxila], coming as the Yona [Greek] envoy (*dūta*) of *Mahārāja* Aṁtalikita [Antialcidas] to the king (*raña*) Kosīputra Bhāgabhadra the Saviour (*trātāra* = Greek 'Soteros'), in the fourteenth year of his prosperous reign (*rājena*).

The three eternal principles, by practising which one is led to [heaven] are: self-restraint (*dama*), liberality (*chāga*) and abjuring bad conduct (*apramāda*).

Note: The most easily accessible reproduction of the text of this famous inscription is perhaps in K.G. Krishnan, *Prakrit and Sanskrit Epigraphs, 257 BC to 320 AD,* Mysore, 1989, pp. 117–18, with photographic reproduction opposite p. 117. The second paragraph above represents a separate part of the inscription. On the reading 'Kosīputra' we have followed D.R. Bhandarkar.

Extract 1.2
Mathura Lion Capital Inscription
(Prakrit in Kharoshṭhī characters)

The chief queen of the *mahakshatrava* Rajula, Ayasia Kamuia, the daughter of crown-prince (*yuvarañа)* Kharaosta, the mother of Nada Diaka, by her, together with her mother Abuhola, her father's mother Pishpasi, her brother Hayuara, with his daughter Hana, the harem (*ateura*) and the almoner's house (? *horaka-parivara*) was established in this piece of land, which is just outside the [*sangharāma*] border, the relic of the lord Shakamuni Budha – after having performed the solemnities over *[Shri]raya* Muki and his horse and a stupa (*thuva*) and a *sagharama* [so spelt] in the acceptance of the order of the four quarters of the Sarvāstivādins (*sarvastivata*).

The crown-prince (*yuvaraya*) Kharaosta, Kamuia, having made prince (*kumara*) Khalamasa (and) Maja, the youngest, assenting parties, by the *mahakshatrava* Rajula's son – the younger brother of Kalui – the *kshatrava* Shuḍasa, Nauluda – by the *kshatrava* Shuḍasa this piece of land, (viz.) the encampment (*kadhavara*) of Veyaūdirna and also the encampment Busapara, limited by Urvarapara, was granted, after having made it (an appurtenance just) outside the limit – as a religious gift (*dhama-dana*) in the cave-monastery (*guha-vihara*) – having given it, with (libations of) water, to the teacher Budhateva [Buddhadeva]: to Budhila from Nakara [Nagara], the *sarvastivata* monk (*bhikhu*) – in honour of *Mahakshatava* Kusula Patika (and) the *kshatava* Mevaki Miyika – in trust of the Sarvastivatas: to the teacher Budhila from Nakara, the Sarvastivata monk (*bhikhu*), a *khalula* (?) to teach the foremost *mahasaghi (Mahāsāṁghikas*), the truth; as honouring of all the Budhas, honouring of the *dhama* [Doctrine], honouring of the *Sagha* [*Saṁgha*, the Monastic Order]; honouring the whole of Sakastana, of the *kshatrava* Khardaa, of Takshila, Kronina, Khalashamusha.

Note: Sten Konow's translation (*Corpus Inscriptionum Indicarum*, Vol. II, Part 1, pp. 30–49) has been followed, with some modifications. In Kharoṣhṭhī long vowels (ā, ī, ū, etc.) are not employed. Almost all names of the Saka chiefs are non-Indian. It is interesting that the traditional Buddhist reference to the Buddha, *dhamma* and *saṁgha* should precede the reference to Sakastana, the Saka homeland.

Extract 1.3
Junagadh Rock Inscription of Rudradāman, AD 150 (Sanskrit)

The lake Sudarshana, from Girinagara [mod. Girnar] . . . of a structure so well-joined as to rival the spur of a mountain, because all its embankments are strong, in breadth, length and height, constructed without gaps as they are of stone. . . . Furnished with a natural dam . . . And with well-provided conduits (*parnālī*), drains and means to guard against foul matter . . . three sections . . . and other favours, is (now) in excellent condition.

This same (lake) – on the first of the dark half of Mārgashīrṣha in the seventy-second – 72nd – year [16 November AD 150] of the king (*rājña*) *mahākṣhatrapa* Rudradāman, whose name is repeated by the venerable, the son of [the king, the *kṣhatrapa,* lord (*svāmi*) Jayadāman] . . . (and) son's son of the king *mahākṣhatrapa svāmi* Chaṣhṭana, the taking of whose name is auspicious. . . . When, by the clouds pouring with rain the earth had been converted, as it were, into one ocean by the excessively swollen floods of the Suvarṇasikatā, Palāshinī and other streams of mount Ūrjayat, the dam (*setu*) [burst] . . . though proper precautions [had been taken], the water – churned by a storm, which, of a most tremendous fury befitting the end of a mundane age (*yuga*), tore down hill-tops, trees, banks, turrets, upper stories, gates and raised places of shelter – scattered, broke to pieces . . . – with stones, trees, bushes and creeping plants scattered about, [the dam] was thus laid open, down to the bottom of the river. By a breach four hundred and twenty cubits (*hasta*) long just as many broad, (and) seventy-five cubits deep, all the water escaped, so that (the lake), almost like a sandy desert, [became] extremely ugly. . . .

. . . For the sake of . . . [the lake had been] ordered to be made by the Vaishya, Puṣhyagupta, the provincial governor (*rāṣhṭriya*) of the Maurya *rājña*, Chandragupta, adorned with conduits (*praṇālī*) for Ashoka the Maurya, by the Yavana *rāja*, Tuṣhāspha; and by the conduit ordered to be made by him, constructed in a manner worthy of a king (and) seen in that breach, the extensive dam (*setu*).

. . . [Of Rudradāman:] he who, because from the womb he was distinguished by the possession of undisturbed, consummate royal fortune (*rāja-lakshmī*), was resorted to by all castes (*sarva varṇa*) and chosen as their lord to protect them; who made the vow, and is true to it to the last breath of his life, to abstain from slaying men, except in battle; who (showed) compassion . . . not failing to deal blows to an equal antagonist meeting him face to face; who grants protection of life to local people (*janapada*) repairing to him of their own accord and those prostrating themselves before him; who is the lord of the towns (*nagara*), marts (*nigama*) and rural districts (*janapada*), which are never troubled by robbers (*dasyu*), snakes, wild beasts, diseases and the like, where all subjects are attached to him [in] the whole of eastern and western Akarāvantī (Akara-and-Avanti), the Anūpa country, Ānarta, Surāshṭra, Shvabhra, Maru, Kachchha, Sindhu-Sauvīra, Kukura, Aparāṁta, Nishāda and other territories gained by his own valour, where through his might the objects of [religion], wealth and pleasure [are daily attained]; who by force destroyed the Yaudheyas who were loath to submit, rendered proud as they were by having manifested the title of heroes among all Kshatriyas; who obtained good repute, because he, in spite of having twice in fair fight completely defeated Sātakarṇi, the lord of Dakshiṇāpatha, on account of the nearness of their connection, did not destroy him; who (obtained) victory . . .; who reinstates deposed kings (*rāja*); who by the right raising of his hand has earned the strong attachment of Dharma; who has attained wide fame by studying and remembering, by the knowledge of grammar (*shabdārtha*), music (*gāndharva*), logic (*nyāya*), and other great sciences (*vidya*); who . . . the management of horses, elephants and chariots, sword and shield, pugilistic combat and other . . . the quickness and efficiency of opposing forces; who, day by day, is in the habit of bestowing presents and honours, whose treasury by the tax (*bali*), tolls (*shulka*) and share [in produce] (*bhāga*), rightfully obtained, overflows with an accumulation of gold, silver, diamonds, beryl stones and (other) precious things; who . . . Prose and verse, which are clear, agreeable, sweet, charming, beautiful, excelling by the proper use of words and adorned; whose beautiful body possesses the most excellent marks and signs, such as length, dimension and height, voice, gait, colour, vigour and strength; who himself has acquired the title of *mahākshatrapa*; who has been wreathed with many garlands at the *syaṁvaras* of rulers' daughters – he, the *mahākshatrapa* Rudradāman, in order to . . . cows and Brāhmaṇas for a thousand years, and to increase his religious merit and fame – without oppressing the people of town and country (*paura-jānapada jana*) by tax (*kara*), forced labour (*vishṭi*) and forced benevolences (*praṇayakriyā*) – by a vast amount of money from his own treasury and in not too long a time made the dam (*setu*) three times as strong in breadth and length . . . (and so) had (this lake) made more beautiful to look at.

When in this matter the *mahakshatrapa's* counsellors (*mati-sachiva*) and executive officials (*karma-sachiva*), who though fully endowed with qualifications of ministers (*amātya*), were averse to a task (considered) futile on account of the enormous extent of the breach, opposed its commencement, (and) when the people (*prajā*) in the despair of having the dam rebuilt were loudly lamenting, (the work) was carried out by the Pahlava, the minister (*amātyā*), Suvishākha, the son of Kulaipa, who for the benefit of the people of town and country (*paura-jānapada jana*) had been appointed by the king in this government to rule the whole of Ānarta and Surāshṭra, – who by his proper dealings (*vyavhāra*) and views in things worldly (*artha*) and spiritual (*dharma*), increased the attachment (of the people); who was able, patient, not wavering, not arrogant, noble (*ārya*) (and) not to be bribed (*ahārya*) (and) who, by his good administration (*svadhitishṭhatā*) increased the spiritual merit, fame and glory of his master.

Note: F. Kielhorn's translation (*Epigraphia Indica*, VIII, pp. 36–49) is here reproduced, with a shift of a long clause and some minor emendations. See *Map 1.2* for such places and regions as are mentioned in this inscription and can be identified. The surface of the rock is worn out or chipped away at places, so there are many gaps in the text.

Although this inscription is conventionally assigned to AD 150, it is worth remembering that 16 November 150 is the date of storm that caused the great breach in the embankment. The inscription was set up later when the repairs had been carried out.

Extract 1.4

Manusmṛiti, Fall of the Yavanas, Shakas and Pahlavas (Chapter X)

43. But in consequence of the omission of the sacred rites and their not consulting Brāhmaṇas, the following tribes of Kshatriyas have gradually sunk in this world to the condition of Shūdras.

44. (Viz.) the Pauṇḍrakas, the Choḍas, the Drāviḍas, the Kāmbojas, the Yavanas, the Shakas, the Pāradas, the Pahlavas, the Chīnas, the Kirātas and the Daradas.

Note: The translation is by G. Bühler. The peoples whose fall into ranks of Shūdras is here celebrated mainly comprise peoples of the north-west (Kāmbojas, Yavanas, Shakas, Pāradas, Pahlavas, Daradas) or of the south (Choḍas, Drāviḍas). The Pauṇḍrakas were inhabitants of Pauṇḍra (north Bangladesh). 'Chīnas' probably means the Chinese, the land-route to whose country lay through the north-west.

This passage reflects a characteristic compound of various cultural, regional and linguistic prejudices. It was obviously composed *after* the eclipse of the power of the Greeks, Parthians and Sakas (Shakas) in north-west India, and this helps to date the *Manusmṟiti* to the second century AD.

Note 1.1
Numismatics

Numismatics as a word is derived from the Greek word *nomisma*, coin or current coin, and therefore means the study of *coins* or metal pieces serving as tokens of money, though it is extended in ordinary use to the study of paper currency notes, medals and other tokens as well. Here we are concerned only with it in its strict sense, viz. the study of coins.

When coins were minted after the fashion of Greek coinage, first of all by the Bactrian Greek and then by the Indo-Greek rulers, these began to supplant the earlier Indian punch-marked coins, on which latter see Note 1.1 in K.M. Shrimali, *The Age of Iron and the Religious Revolution,* in our series. The kinds of coins that came with the Greeks are still with us (at least for small cash), and have certain common characteristics which may first be described.

The three standard metals in which coins are issued are *gold* (numismatic symbol: A/), *silver* (AR) and *copper* (Æ). When silver and copper are combined, the alloy is called *billon*, and usually acquires a black appearance. Copper mixed with nickel is termed *cupro-nickel.* Another alloy is *potin* (copper alloyed with tin, lead and zinc). In the period covered by this volume, nickel and lead also came to be used in coins. The punch-marked coins used to be of various shapes; but the coins minted by the Greeks were usually circular, squarish shapes being sometimes adopted later, apparently to suit Indian familiarity with rectangular punch-marked coins.

Numismatists call the two sides of a coin 'obverse' and 'reverse'. When the hammer struck the metal piece that was to be turned into coin, the side of the piece underneath, which attains its shape from the die on the anvil and so tends to be convex, is called **obverse.** The other side, which receives its shape from the die fixed to the punch or hammer, is called **reverse**. In addition to these technical senses of the two terms, the side which contains the bust or representation of the sovereign or the chief device and lettering is normally called 'obverse', and the other side, 'reverse'. This mode of classification becomes necessary in the case of coins that are cast in moulds, where the side struck by the hammer cannot naturally be identified. In some cases it is possible that the 'obverse' by one definition may be 'reverse' by another;

but in such cases the primary technical definition based on the lower and upper dies for 'obverse' and 'reverse' should, perhaps, prevail.

Any writing or phrase or name impressed on the coin is called a **legend.** These legends usually give the name and titles of the sovereign and occasionally further information, such as the ruler's father's name. By the way the letters are written one can also establish, with the aid of Palaeography, the period to which they belong. Moreover, bilingual coin-legends offer an aid to the decipherment of ancient scripts. The decipherment of both the Brāhmī and Kharoshṭhī scripts began in the 1830s with the reading of Greek rulers' names in their bilingual coin-legends.

In the early Bactrian and Indo-Greek coins the rulers' **portraits** on the obverse were remarkably realistic, and this fact has led to speculations about lengths of reigns of some rulers based on their portraits at different stages of life, or about their family affinities based on their facial features. But as the busts on later coins became more stylized, such inferences cannot be attempted, though different headgears could still be of some significance. Images of divinities, usually found on the reverse, can be taken to reflect the rulers' or their subjects' religious attachments. Coins also contain symbols, some clearly affiliated to particular rulers, which identify their coins even when the sovereigns' names cannot be read. The dates in years that begin to be shown on coins of the Satraps of Gujarat after AD 180 are a great aid to reconstructing dynastic chronology; but this custom remained unique to this dynasty during our period.

Sometimes coins of one ruler are found *counter-struck* by the dies of another ruler. This generally implies that the two rulers were either contemporaries, or the counter-striking ruler succeeded the original issuer by inheritance, coup or conquest. Counter-striking saves minting costs, particularly in the case of coins of cheaper metal like copper; it has little to do with the state of abundance or scarcity of the metal at the time. But when an entire treasury was appropriated by the victor, as in the case of the Nasik (Jogathembi) hoard of Nahapāna's silver coins of which 9,270 were counter-struck by Gotamīputa Satakaṇi, the urgent need to spend or distribute the booty probably dictated the short-cut, since fresh minting after melting down the coins would have taken a great deal of time.

Each coin, by its metal and weight, represented a unit of money whose name is not usually indicated on the coins themselves. The Bactrian Greek rulers issued drachmas of gold and silver according to the standard Attic weight of 4.27 grammes, while later Greek rulers followed for their silver issues, containing Kharoshṭhī legends, the 'Indian' weight for the drachma, viz. 3.75 grammes only. The Western Satraps' silver coins usually weighed 2.33 grammes or thereabouts.

Each coin, at the time of issue, had to include in its value the price of the metal carried in it, plus the *mintage* or cost of minting, and *seigniorage* or the ruler's profit. If the mintage was open or 'free', then all merchants bringing uncoined metal (*bullion*) to the mint had to bring in metal of a weight larger than that of the coin sought, in order to cover both mintage and seigniorage. Each coin, before being worn out, should therefore normally have borne value above the market price of its metallic content. When a coin's value was thus established, rulers might have the temptation to resort to **debasement**, which usually meant maintaining the weight of the coin but replacing in part the higher-value metal with an inferior metal – e.g. through reducing the silver-content of a silver coin by alloying it with copper. Though initially the state might gain by saving on silver while meeting its obligations in debased currency, treating it as of the same value as enjoyed by the purer coin, ultimately it would itself have to accept the same coin in tax payments at its fictitious value, and so its initial gains would be cancelled. Moreover, **counterfeiting** always becomes easier and more profitable with debased coinage if it is artificially sought to be kept at a higher value. In general, coin debasement (like the overprinting of paper currency notes by modern states) took place when the normal tax collections of the state did not suffice to meet its expenditure. Such a situation might arise, for example, if the state lost tax resources as a consequence of losing parts of its previous territorial possessions, or faced persistent threats to its security, calling for larger military expenditure, or, again, suffered from a breakdown in internal administration. It might also resort to debasement because of a rise in the price of the original money-metal: there have been suggestions of world-wide silver scarcities at different periods of time. In other words, there are many factors to be considered before one can fix on the cause for the debasement of coinage by an issuing state.

Sometimes, in numismatists' discussions of the effects of debasement, a principle called *Gresham's law* is mentioned. Named after Sir John Gresham (1519–79), this law simply states that 'bad money' drives 'good money' out of the market. Here bad money means debased coins and 'good money', coins with better metallic content. When the debased coins carry the same nominal value, e.g. in debt repayment or tax payment, as the good coins, people prefer to make their legal payments in bad money and send the good money abroad where coins are accepted only at their true metallic value. People even smelt down good coins to obtain the metal they contain, which can then be sold at a higher market value in debased currency. Thus it is the debased money alone which remains in use within the territory of the state concerned.

Note 1.2
Bibliographical Note

The two major works on the Bactrian Greek and Indo-Greek rulers are W.W. Tarn's highly speculative *The Greeks in Bactria and India*, second edition, Cambridge, 1951, and A.K. Narain's possibly overcritical *The Indo-Greeks*, Oxford, 1957. Many of the two authors' arguments have now to be largely revised in the light of the remarkable epigraphic and archaeological discoveries which took place within two decades of the publication of their works. For a more updated account, see P. Bernard's contribution (Chapter 4) in Janos Harmatta (ed.), *History of Civilizations of Central Asia* (UNESCO), II, Paris, 1994. Those interested in sorting out the problems of Bactrian Greek and Indo-Greek coinage will find their basic material brought together in A.N. Lahiri's comprehensive *Corpus of Indo-Greek Coins*, Calcutta, 1965.

On the Sakas (Shakas) and Parthians (Pahlavas) of the north-west, see chapter 8 by B.N. Puri in the *History of Civilizations of Central Asia*, Vol. II, above cited. On the Satraps of Western India (the Shaka rulers of Gujarat), a detailed account was furnished by Edward James Rapson in the Introduction (pp. xcii–clvii) to his *Catalogue of the Coins of the Andhra Dynasty, the Western Kṣatrapas*, & c., London, 1908 (reprint, 1967). It needs to be updated, which purpose is largely served by Ajay Mitra Shastri, *The Sātavāhanas and the Western Kshatrapas,* Nagpur, 1998, pp. 133–74. Satya Shrava, *Sakas in India,* New Delhi, 1981, has some useful documentation, but is badly organized and, in parts, highly uncritical.

The Saka (Shaka) rulers are represented by a number of Kharoshṭhī and Brāhmī inscriptions. For the text and translations of inscriptions in Kharoshṭhī, see Sten Konow, *Kharoshṭhī Inscriptions (Corpus Inscriptionum Indicarum*, Vol. II, Pt. 1), Calcutta, 1929 (reprint, New Delhi, 1991). In *Epigraphia Indica,* Vol. VIII, 1905–06, were published critically edited texts and translations of the Nasik cave inscriptions of the reign of the *kshatrapa* Nahapāna, and the opposing Sātavāhana rulers (pp. 59–96), and the famous Junagadh rock inscription of Rudradāman (pp. 36–49) (our *Extract 1.3*). A comprehensive collection of inscriptions of the period as a whole, with texts and summaries, is by K.G. Krishnan (ed.), *Prakrit and Sanskrit Epigraphs, 257 BC to 320 AD*, Mysore, 1989. Strangely, it omits the Mathura lion-capital inscription; otherwise the coverage is admirable.

With reference to our *Note 1.1* on Numismatics, the reader may consult two general textbooks: C.J. Brown, *The Coins of India*, London, 1922, an old but still serviceable text; and Parmeshwari Lal Gupta, *Coins*, NBT, New Delhi, 1996/2000, – a fairly reliable guide to the history of Indian coinages.

Two references, perhaps, need especially to be provided, for two facts of some significance, the first for chronology and the other for military history. Percy Gardner, in *The Coins of the Greek and Scythic Kings of Bactria and India in the British Museum*, London, 1886 (Indian reprint, New Delhi, 1971), pp. xlvi–xlvii, in a rarely noticed observation, notes the chronological implications of changes in the forms of certain Greek letters in the coins of Saka and Parthian rulers; and Max Sparreboom draws attention to the absence of the horse-bit in early Ancient India, in *Indo-Iranian Journal*, Vol. 29 (2), 1986, p. 127.

2

The Shungas, Kalinga, the Sātavāhanas and South India

2.1 The Shungas

The *Purāṇas* (on which see *Note 2.1*) tell us that Bṛihadratha, the last Mauryan king, was overthrown by his commander-in-chief (*senānīr*), Pushyamitra. This event, if the *Purāṇas* are right in giving the Mauryas a period of rule of 137 years, should have occurred in 185 BC (taking 322 BC to be the approximate date of Chandragupta Maurya's accession). That the usurper was indeed the commander-in-chief is confirmed by the Ayodhya inscription (late first century BC) of Dhanadeva, who, while claiming the title of *dharma-rāja* for himself, says he was sixth in descent from *senāpatī* Pushpamitra (so spelt). The inscription further credits Pushpamitra with two *ashvamedhas* or horse-sacrifices, a challenging royal ritual henceforth undertaken by rulers pretending to any position of power. The grammarian Patañjali (*c.* 150 BC) also refers to Vedic sacrifices performed for Pushyamitra. His *ashvamedha* is a central event in Kālidāsa's play *Mālavikāgnimitra*, which has Agnimitra, the son of Pushyamitra (so also by the Purāṇic list), as its hero. Whether the conflict with the Yavana king that this play describes is the same as the one Patañjali had in mind when he speaks of the Yavana besieging Sāketa and Madhyāmika (see *Chapter 1.1*) is uncertain, because it is quite risky to treat the *Mālavikāgnimitra*, written over 500 years later, as a genuine source of history.

Unlike the Greek, Saka and Parthian dynasties whose rulers issued coins with their names stamped on them, the Shungas appear to have continued using and minting punch-marked coins, so that none of the rulers listed in the *Purāṇas* has left any coins attributable to him. Certain relevant inscriptions are not dated, but palaeographic features help us to establish a rough sequence. The earliest of these inscriptions is the Besnagar (Vidisha) pillar inscription of Heliodorus (*Extract 1.1*). Heliodorus was the envoy of Taxila's Greek ruler Antialcidas to the court of *raña* Bhāgabhadra, who had reigned fourteen years when the inscription was set up. If the *Purāṇas* were Sanskritizing Prakrit names in popular tradition on their own, Bhāgavata in their list, with a reign of thirty-two years (which, by one count based on the *Purāṇas*, would correspond to 115–83 BC), could well be identical with Bhāgabhadra. If the latter name was spelt Bhāgabada in popular Prakrit, it could be held also to be a variant of Bhāgavata and so germinate a wrong Purāṇic restoration. By this time, then, Vidisha in Malwa (near Sanchi) must have become the Shuṅga capital.

There are inscriptions at Bharhut, datable to first century BC, two of which expressly refer to the current 'rule of the Suga' (*Suganam raje*), i.e. of the Shuṅga dynasty. One of these belongs to the *raño* Visadeva, whose grandson Dhanabhūtī had set it up. From another inscription we learn that Dhanabhūtī himself became *rāja,* with his son Vādhapāla as *kumāra*. Clearly, the Shuṅga administration here was losing out to a local line of rulers who did not even care to mention the name of their Shuṅga overlord.

Finally, there is the Sanskrit inscription of Dhanadeva, son of Phalgudeva, from Ayodhya – already mentioned. Although he claims to be the sixth in line of descent from Pu<u>sh</u>yamitra ('Pu<u>sh</u>pamitra'), his name does not occur in the Purāṇic list. Nor does he, indeed, pretend to be anything more than the ruler of Kosala (*Kosalādhipī*). Clearly, by this time the Shuṅga dominions had broken up, with Vidisha, perhaps, already lost to the Kāṇvas, the next dynasty according to the *Purāṇas*, and other parts passing under local rulers, of whose existence we sometimes learn from coins and inscriptions (see below).

Pu<u>sh</u>yamitra, the founder of the Shuṅga dynasty, is accused in the Buddhist *Divyāvadāna* of hostility to Buddhism and of destroying Buddhist *vihāras*. There is no way in which this can be verified. At least the Bharhut *stupa* and its gates and railings were apparently built in Shuṅga times, and there is epigraphic evidence to this effect. But whether connected with a Brahmanical revival or not, some change had taken place in outlook. One indication of this has been noted by Harry Falk, namely an anxiety about purity of caste manifested in a new royal concern: the woman who had borne the ruler needed to be of a spotless

Brahman *gotra* (kin-group). Heliodorus's Besnagar inscription (*Extract 1.1*) carefully names the ruler to whose court he had been sent as 'Kosīputra Bhāgabhadra', i.e. Bhāgabhadra, the son of a Brahman mother of the Kautsi *gotra*. Dhanabhūtī, the Shuṅga-period princeling at Bharhut, records, first, the *gotra* of his mother (Vāchchi = Vātsī), and then only, the name of his father; the *gotra* of his father's mother (Gotī = Gauptī) now follows, and only thereafter the name of his grandfather, the local ruler; and, finally, the *gotra* of his great grand-mother (Gāgī = Gārgī). In his Ayodhya inscription, Pushyamitra's descendant, the Kosala ruler Dhanadeva, is careful to describe himself as 'Kaushikī-putra', claiming thereby that his mother was a Brahman woman of Kaushikī *gotra*. This concern with the mother being a Brahman in a polygamous society, where a ruler's wives could belong to various *varṇas*, implies an expectation of political prestige to be gained if the ruler could lay claim to having unsullied Brahman blood from his womb. It was surely one political reflection of the increasing caste consciousness and diffusion of the caste order which so deeply marks post-Mauryan times.

2.2 Kaliṅga and Local Dynasties of Northern India

The famous Hathigumpha rock inscription of **Khāravela** in Orissa has brought to light the existence of a powerful kingdom, that of Kaliṅga. The inscription (*Extract 2.2*) is unique in setting out, in the form of annals, a narrative of what happened in the thirteen successive years of the reign of Khāravela, the *Kaliṅgādhipati* ('Kaliṅga ruler'). It is datable from its internal evidence: it puts the Nandas (of Magadha) 300 years before its time, and so should be placed at *c*. 20 BC at the latest, a date which also suits its script's place in the palaeographic sequence. By this time, as we have seen, the Shuṅga empire had been replaced by the Kāṇvas and by several local principalities. Yet Khāravela himself belongs to a period early enough when, like the Shuṅgas, he was not still called upon to issue coins with written legends in his name as a mark of sovereignty.

Khāravela, by his own statement, belonged to the Mahāmeghavāhana dynasty. We have no means of knowing when Kaliṅga, which had been annexed to the Mauryan empire in Ashoka's 8th regnal year (*c*. 262 BC), again became a separate kingdom, and when the

Mahāmeghavāhana dynasty established itself within it. Khāravela's inscription gives us few indications of the extent of his kingdom. Its own site in the Udayagiri hills is close to Tosali, the Mauryan capital of Kaliṅga which is situated within the Mahanadi delta. In the same Udayagiri hills, another Mahāmeghavāhana ruler, Vakadapa, has left an inscription claiming to be the 'Kaliṅgādhipati'. The same overlordship over Kaliṅga is also asserted by Sada, who has left an inscription at Guntupalle, south of the Godavari river. Thus the Kaliṅga kingdom could have stretched deep into modern coastal Andhra; and this makes possible the identification of Khāravela's capital Kaliṅga-nagara, which had suffered from a storm and so might have been near the coast, with the port town of Kalingapatam (in Srikakulam district, Andhra Pradesh)

Given such an extent, one can understand Khāravela's ambitions to conquer other parts of 'Bharadhavasa', one of the earliest references to the name of our country, Bhāratavar<u>sh</u>a. (His chief queen, in her own cave inscription in the Udayagiri hills, calls him the Kaliṅga *chakavatin*, perhaps the first epigraphic use of the epithet *chakravartin* (the universal conqueror). More specifically, Khāravela speaks of his raids in the Deccan into Sātavāhana (Sātakaṁni's) territory, reaching Asika on the upper Kri<u>sh</u>ṇa river, and of subduing the Bhojakas and Raṭhikas in the upper Godavari valley and Vidarbha. He claims to have devastated Rājagaha (Rājag<u>ri</u>ha) in Bihar and, marching through Magadha, to have made his elephants bathe in the Gaṅgā. He also claims to have driven away a Yavana ruler back to Madhura (Mathura). In the south, he broke an ancient concourse of 'Tramira' (Tamil or Dravida) states, and obtained jewels and pearls from the Paṁḍa (Pāṇḍiya) ruler. Whether all these exploits really took place in the manner described, there is no means of knowing or confirming, for Khāravela remains unknown to us from any source other than his own inscription and that of his queen.

On his administration, the Hathigumpha inscription yields some credible information. His sources of revenue included not only the wealth (*vasu*) exacted from his enemies, but also *kara* (taxes) and *vaṇa* (tolls) imposed on his subjects. He says he granted certain remissions in these, along with various privileges, to various '*jātis* (castes) of the *porajānapada*'. The last term corresponds to *paurajānapada*, 'people of cities and provinces', which occurs in the *Arthashāstra* of Kauṭilya (see *Mauryan India* in this series, Chapter 3.2). In Kauṭilya's work, the *paurajānapada* are not ordinary people but classes through which the localities were governed; and this sense suits the use of this term here, as well as in Rudradāman's Junagadh inscription (see *Chapter 1.3* above). That the *paurajānapada* comprised various castes (*jātis*) is what we would expect, as the caste system had now spread widely over the land.

Khāravela puts his army in four branches, viz. cavalry (*haya*), elephants (*gaja*), infantry (*nara*) and chariots (*ratha*). Perhaps being placed fourth meant that chariots were now losing their importance.

Among the items, other than those of the army, on which Khāravela spent his ample resources, the construction of Mahāvijaya palace came first, with an expenditure of 3,800,000 (copper coins?); next came the restoration of walls and buildings in storm-battered Kaliṁganagara, involving 3,500,000 coins in expenditure. On other repairs and building works the amount of money spent is not stated, but it is significant that much of the work undertaken was concerned with tanks and embankments as at Kaliṁganagara. Khāravela claims to have restored a canal (*paṇādī*) from Tansuliya (not located) to (Kaliṁga-) nagara, that is said to have been built by a Nanda ruler 300 years earlier. Here, again, there is some parallel to Rudradāman's rebuilding of a Mauryan reservoir (Sudarshana lake) on the other side of the peninsula over 150 years later.

Khāravela's religious affiliations are publicly affirmed: he was a follower of Jainism, and the Hathigumpha inscription by its references to Jain monks, their texts ('*Aṁgas* of the sixty-four letters') and ritual, as well as to a Jina image brought back from Magadha, make it an important document for the history of Jainism. His Jain affiliation did not, however, prevent him from stating, in phraseology reminiscent of that of Ashoka's Rock Edict XII, that he gave respectful attention to all sects (*sava-pāsaṁḍa-pūjako*). Indeed he boasts of giving certain tax exemption to Brahmans. Refreshingly, his chief queen, who also donated a cave to a Jain ascetic, claims not a Brāhmaṇa *gotra*, but a royal lineage.

The **Kāṇvas,** whom the Purāṇas hold to be the successors of the Shuṅgas, are unattested by either inscriptions or coinage, and so

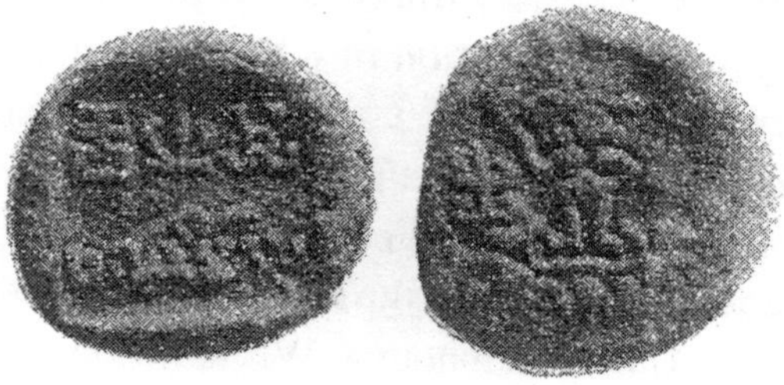

1

2

3

FIGURE 2.1 Copper coins of (1) Phalgunimitra of Pāñchāla; (2) Nava of Kausambi; (3) Sivapalita of Ayodhya.

even the area where they ruled cannot be established. It is obvious from the Hathigumpha inscription of Khāravela that in his time in the Gangā basin, there was no longer a single dominant state: there was Bahastimita, *rāja* of Magadha, and a 'Yavana' *rāja* at Mathura (on the latter, see *Chapter 1.1* above). We otherwise know, as we have seen, that belonging to the line of Pushpamitra (Pushyamitra), there was a separate ruler of Kosala, Dhanadeva. While the Shuṅgas issued no coins – at least, no coins other than legendless punch-marked coins – there begins to be numismatic evidence for at least some local dynasties with a number of rulers whose names appear on their coins (*Figure 2.1*). These were mostly of copper alloy, and, while initially made only by casting, the use of dies gradually spread. Such dynasties have been located in **Kosala**, where Dhanadeva in fact is a name that appears on both cast and die-struck coins. Another line was established in Vatsa or the region around **Kausambi**, in whose vicinity coins of Dhanabhūtī, the local ruler known through Bharhut inscriptions, have been found. A much larger number of coins of rulers, attributed to the kingdom of **Pāñchāla**, have been found in western Uttar Pradesh. At least one of the rulers, Vangapāla, is mentioned in an inscription at Pabhosa near Kausambi. The successive rulers' names given there exhibit what by now had become an established custom, viz. mentioning the *gotra* of the ruler's Brahman mother. Thus we have Vangapāla described as Shaunakāyanīputra, and his son and grandson having similar prefixes (Tevaṇiputra, Vaihidariputra). Another line of rulers was established at Erich, south of the Yamuna river: one of the rulers represented on the coins, Dānamitra of the Baimbaka family, has left an inscription at Erich and another at Musanagar. Another line of similar local rulers, established at Eran and **Vidisha**, is known only from coins.

The primitive technology of coinage and shapes of letters in the short Brāhmī legends suggest that the coins belong to the first century BC and first century AD, during which the issuing rulers are to be placed. Beyond this, it is hard to go; it is equally difficult to establish an order of sequence among the rulers whose names the coins bear.

2.3 The Sātavāhanas

The *Purāṇas* style the Sātavāhana dynasty as **Andhra**, and speak of the Andhra community (Andhra-*jāti*) as one whose members formed the main body of the followers of the dynasty's founder, Shishuka. But the fact is that the inscriptions and most coin find-spots of the early Sātavāhanas are located in Maharashtra. In its own inscriptions, the dynastic name given throughout is Sātavāhana or Sādavāhana. The founder's actual name was Simuka Sātavāhana according to a cave inscription at Nanaghat pass (northern Maharashtra), which, though much damaged, can have its contents partly recovered by the accompanying image-label inscriptions (the images themselves have disappeared). It was set up by queen (*devī*) Nāyanikā, wife of the king Siri Sātakani, son of Simuka-Sātavāhana and lord of the Deccan (*Dakhinapatha-pati*). Her own father was a *Mahāraṭha* (chief); and she was now ruling on behalf of her son, Vedisiri. (Her earlier high position under Siri Sātakani has been reinforced by the discovery of a unique silver coin, which, apart from the ruler's name, bears also hers in its fuller form, Nāganikāya.) Palaeographically, the Nanaghat inscription is placed in the late first century BC. Siri Sātakani is identifiable with Shrī Shātakarṇi, the third king in the Purāṇic list (see *Extract 2.1*). The second ruler, K<u>ri</u>s<u>h</u>ṇa, in the same list is mentioned as 'Kanha of the Sādavāhana family (*kula*)' in a Nasik cave inscription. The rough contemporaneity of these inscriptions, by their script, with the Hathigumpha inscription suggests that Siri-Sātakani is the same as Satakaṁni of that inscription, mentioned as the king who controlled the city of Asika on the Kanha-beṁṇa (Kri<u>sh</u>ṇa-Venna) river somewhere around the south Maharashtra and Karnataka border (see *Extract 2.2*). An inscription recording a donation by a foreman (*āvesani*) of Rano Siri Sātakani at Sanchi could also refer to this king, though it does not necessarily imply that Sanchi was within his dominions since the foreman could well have been a pilgrim. The *Purāṇas*' list shows another Shātakarṇi coming to the throne twenty-eight years after Siri Sātakarṇi, and he is assigned a reign of 56 years. For all we know, he could be the one mentioned in the Hathigumpha and Sanchi inscriptions.

It is difficult to trace the subsequent history of the dynasty since the Purāṇic list does not appear to accord with our other evidence. For example, the reign of Vedisiri, son of Siri-Sātakani, attested by the Nanaghat inscriptions, is nowhere mentioned in the Purāṇic list. It is similarly difficult to identity 'the elder Saraganus' and his successor

Sandanes, described by the *Periplus* of the Eyrthraean Sea, Section 52 (pre-AD 106), as rulers over the Konkan port of Kalyan, with any two rulers mentioned in the *Purāṇas*. An effort has been made to identify Sandanes with Sundara Shātakarni, but he is assigned only one year's reign in the Purāṇas.

The fortunes of the Sātavāhanas appear to have witnessed a rebirth with **Gotamīputa Sātakaṇi** (Gautamīputra of the *Purāṇas*). The name reminds us of the Brahmanizing tendency we had noticed among the later Shuṅgas. Gotamīputa's mother appears in the Nasik inscription, a translation of which is given in our *Extract 2.3*, as Gotami Balasirī, a Brahman woman of the Gautam *gotra*. Though the *Purāṇas* assign the Sātavāhana family to the Andhra *jāti*, by now the dynasty firmly entertained Brahmanical pretensions, and the incorporation of the mother's *gotra* in the king's name was a means whereby one's purity of blood as a Brahman could be proclaimed. The Nasik inscription underlines this by claiming that Gotamīputa, himself a 'unique Brahman', 'crushed the pride and conceit of the Khatiyas (Kshatriyas)', and that he also 'stopped the admixture of the four *vanas (varṇas*)' – the first reference in any inscription to this kingly duty.

The political feats which Gotamīputa performed in restoring 'the glory of the Sātavāhana family' are also proudly recounted. One of these was the uprooting of 'the Khakarata race', which must refer to the overthrow of the Shaka *mahākshatrapa* Nahapāna's power, centred at Nasik. (This event has already been described in *Chapter 1.3*.) After overthrowing Nahapāna, Gotamīputa laid claim to a number of territories named in the Nasik cave inscription, extending beyond the Narmada up to Akra-Avati (Akra and Avanti, or Malwa). Gotamīputa counterstruck some 9,000 or more silver coins of Nahapāna found in the Nasik hoard; and this and the Sātavāhana inscriptions at Nasik confirm the finality of Gotamīputa Sātakani's success against Nahapāna. Neither the dates in Nahapāna's inscriptions nor the regnal years mentioned in Gotamīputa's can be keyed to any known era. Given what we know about Gujarat's Shaka ruler Rudradāman's conflicts and contacts with Gotamīputa's successors, Gotamīputa is best placed in the last quarter of the first century AD. Gotamīputa has left behind two inscriptions in the Nasik caves, one of his 18th regnal year, the other of the 24th. Obviously, therefore, he reigned for a longer period than the twenty-one years allowed to him by the *Purāṇas*.

Gotamīputa's son, Pulumāvi ('Puloma' in the Purāṇic list), also had his Brahmanical credentials strengthened by being designated 'Vāsiṭhiputa', i.e. son born of a Brahman mother of Vasiṣhṭha *gotra*. Ptolemy (writing, AD 146–70) has an entry for the town of Baithana, identified with Paithan in Maharashtra, which he describes as 'the royal seat of Ptolemaios or Polemaios', the latter name being taken to represent Pulumāvi. It could well be so since the time broadly suits that ruler, but there is no other indication that Paithan was Pulomāvi's capital. The find-spots of his inscriptions – Nasik, Karle, Amaravati, Myakadoni, Sannathi, Banavasi and Vasana – offer good evidence for the large extent the Sātavāhana dominions had now acquired, stretching across the peninsula and practically including the whole of Maharashtra and Andhra and the northern half of Karnataka. The inscriptions at Nasik carry as dates his regnal years 2, 6, 19 and 22, while at Karle they are dated to regnal years 7 and 24, and at Myakadoni, regnal year 8. He had, therefore, a respectable length of period as ruler as well: the *Purāṇas* give him twenty-eight years of reign, which would encompass all his dated inscriptions.

Pulumāvi does not use the name Sātakani in his inscriptions; and it is therefore likely that when Rudradāman, in his Junagadh inscription of AD 150, speaks of twice defeating 'Sātakarṇi, the lord of Dakṣhināpatha', his reference is to Vāsiṣhṭhīputra Sātakarṇi, who is represented on some rare silver portrait coins, besides lead coins with his name-legend only (*Figure 2.2*), and is mentioned in his queen's Kanheri inscription. This queen describes herself as the daughter of Mahākṣhatrapa Ru(dradāman) – a fact that explains Rudradāman's acknowledgement (in the Junagadh inscription) of the closeness of his relationship with his defeated adversary. It is possible, then, that by AD 150 the Sātavāhanas had lost all territory north of the present Maharashtra border to the Shaka satraps of Gujarat.

Among the later Sātavāhana rulers, the one whose inscriptions are most numerous is Gotamīputa Sāmi Siriyaña Sātakaṇi (Sanskrit: Gautamīputra Svāmi Shrī-Yajña Shātakarṇi). He is represented at Nasik by an inscription of his 7th regnal year; at Kanheri by two inscriptions, one of which is of his 16th year; and one at China in Krishna district, coastal Andhra, of his 27th year. He thus maintained control over both Maharashtra and Andhra. The *Purāṇas* make him ascend the throne ten or fourteen years after the end of the reign of Pulumāvi ('Puloma'), and assign him a reign of twenty-nine years, which, given the dates of his inscriptions, is worthy of some credit. He may thus be placed in the later decades of the second century AD.

Siriyaña Sātakaṇi was probably the last ruler who maintained control over the bulk of the Sātavāhana dominions. According to the *Purāṇas*, the dynasty came to a close twenty-three years after his death, with the last ruler 'Pulomāvi' ruling for seven years. He, in all likelihood, is the same as the Pulamāvi referred to in an inscription at Myakadoni in Bellary district, Karnataka.

The Sātavāhanas were apparently not the earliest rulers in the Deccan who issued coins with written legends, being preceded in this by some local rulers. But their coinage, to judge from find-spots and numbers, had a far more extensive range. The metals they normally used were lead and copper alloys. Their silver coinage is exceptionally rare and begins only after Gotamīputa Sātakaṇi. They seem to have been influenced by the sight of Roman or Shaka coinage, because their coins bear the rulers' portraits as well. Another feature of the later Sātavāhana coinage is the presence of legends in two languages, Prakrit in Brahmi on the obverse and irregular Tamil in the Tamil-Brahmi script on the reverse (*Figure 2.2*).

On the Sātavāhana **administration**, our knowledge is limited to information and inferences derived from a few inscriptions, mainly those of the Nasik and Karle caves. A general name for their officials seems to have been *amacha* (Sanskrit: *amātya*); they were posted at different towns (like Govardhana near Nasik) or entrusted with keeping records of public transactions, such as the award of royal land-grants. A still higher officer seems to have been *mahāraṭhi* (Sanskrit *mahārāshtrin*), 'a great governor of a region (*rāshṭra*)'. One *Mahāraṭhi* Sadakana (Sātakaṇi) Kalalāya even issued coins of his own in lead. It is a matter of speculation whether this term was also related to the geographical territory of the Raṭhikas (*Map 3.1*) and so to the region that was later called *Mahārāshṭra*. There also seems to have been in use an analogous term, 'Mahābhoja', as the title of governor. Finally, we have

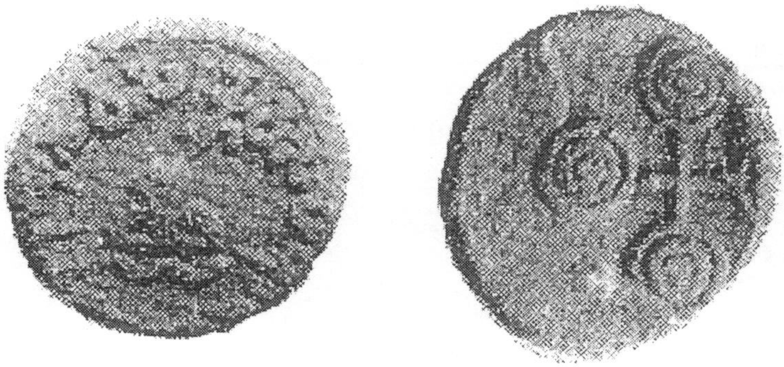

1

2

FIGURE 2.2 (1) Lead coin of Vāsiṭhiputa Siri Pulumāvi (P.L. Gupta); **(2) Silver coin of Gotamiputa Siri Yāna Sātakaṇi: note portrait and 'irregular Tamil' legend** (C.J. Brown).

the official called *mahā-senāpati*, which, to judge from the literal meaning of the word, must have been the designation of the commander-in-chief of the army. In one inscription, the district (*ahāra*) of Sātavahani (Bellary district, Karnataka) is described as a *mahā-senāpati*'s *janapada,* suggesting that particular territories used to be assigned to high officials for their income (see *Extract 4.3*).

Map 2.1 The Peninsula

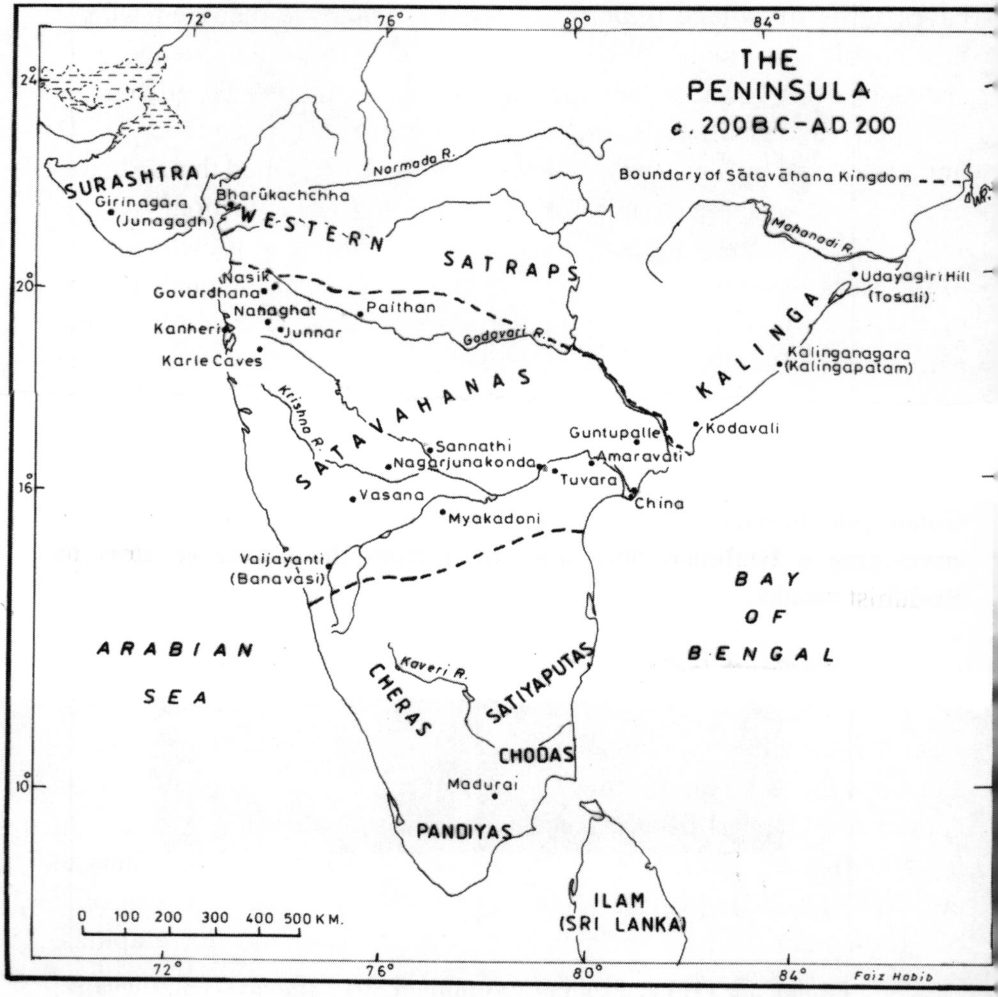

About taxation, especially the revenue obtained from land, we have hardly any clue to go by. In inscriptions at the Nasik and Karle caves, gifts of village (*gāma*) and field (*kheta*) are recorded where, presumably, the grantee obtained the right to claim state revenue. It is stated in a set formula that the land-grant was not to be entered or 'touched' (by tax officials), nor were salt-digs to be made there or the grantees vexed by local (*raṭha*) levies. It is to be presumed that ordinary peasant-land was subject to all these four sources of extortion.

We have commented above on the Brahman transformation of the Sātavāhana dynasty. But it is important to enter the qualification that such caste addiction did not prevent expression of faith in and patronage of Buddhism. In the very inscription in the Nasik caves in which Gotamīputa's Brahman status is proclaimed, his mother, in whose Brahman *gotra* he took pride, records a grant to the Buddhist monks of the Bhadāyanīya sect, the 'merit' of this being dedicated to Gotamīputa himself (*Extract 2.3*). Clearly, no contradiction was seen in envisaging a Brahman obtaining merit from the giving of alms to Buddhist monks.

2.4 South India

The earliest evidence for state formation in south India comes from Megasthenes (*c.* 300 BC), who, as quoted by Arrian (*Indica*, VIII–IX), says that a kingdom ruled over by queen Pandaia in (south) India contained rich pearl fisheries. We have here an undoubted reference to the **Pāṇḍiya** kingdom and the Tuticorin pearl fisheries. The Mauryan emperor Ashoka, in his Rock Edict II of *c.* 258 BC, records the despatch of missions to Choḍas, Paṁḍiyas, Satiyaputas and Keralaputas, whereas in his Rock Edict XIII (*c.* 257 BC), only the **Choḍas** and Paṁḍiyas are mentioned, suggesting that at the time these were the two more important states of the south. The traditional area of the Choḍas (Tamil: Choḷas) was the Kaveri delta, whereas that of the Paṁḍiyas or Pāṇḍiyas (Tamil: Pāṇṭiyas) was the district around Madurai. The Keralaputas are identified with Cheramāṉ (Cheras) whose original seat was in the Coimbatore district of Tamil Nadu, while the Satiyaputas are represented by Tamil Atiyan, the name of a dynasty dominant in the region around Pondicherry.

The Tamil Brāhmī inscriptions, which date from the second

century BC onward, have only stray data about rulers and chiefs; and from these little political history can be reconstructed. The confirmation of the identification of **Satiyaputa** with Atiyan by the Jambai inscription is, however, quite an important aid to us. These inscriptions also show that Jain monks were recipients of considerable donations from officials and local chiefs, a recording of such gifts being the main concern of most of the early inscriptions.

It is mainly the **Shaṅgam** (Chankam) texts of the first to the third centuries AD (see *Note 2.2*) on the basis of which efforts have been made to reconstruct dynastic histories of the south, partly by stripping the poems of their exaggerations and inflated descriptions. By and large, it is the **Cheras** about whom we learn the most, especially about their conquests, often reputedly carried 'up to the Himalayas'! The Chera rulers could have been the leading figures in the Tramira (Dravida or Tamil) *dah-saṁghāta*, the regional league as it were, which Khāravela, the Kalinga ruler, in his Hathigumpha inscription, claims to have broken up (*Extract 2.2*). The Roman author Pliny the Elder (d. AD 79) and the Greek work *Periplus* (pre-106) refer to the Chera kingdom respectively as 'Caelobothras' and 'Cerobotras', which remind us of the Ashokan edict's 'Keralaputas'. A particularly powerful ruler in Shaṅgam texts is said to have been Peruñcheral Irampurai, who overthrew the Satiyaputas (see below). Chera rulers issued copper coins with Tamil-Brahmi legends in the first century AD and even silver portrait coins in the third century. Their capital seems to have been at Karur.

Most of the early Tamil-Brahmi inscriptions are concentrated around Madurai ('Mattirai'), which was the Pāṇḍiya capital (*Map 4.2c*). A 'Paṁḍa' (Pāṇḍiya) ruler sent gifts of pearls to Khāravela (*Extract 2.2*), thus apparently breaching the Tamil league with which Khāravela had entered into conflict. In the first century AD, Pliny (d. 79) mentions the kingdom of 'Pandion' with its capital at 'Modura' (Madurai), while the *Periplus* makes the 'Pandion' king master of the pearl fisheries. Two victorious Pāṇḍiya rulers bear the name Neṭuñcheḷiyaṇ in the Shaṅgam texts, and the name also occurs in the Tamil-Brahmi inscriptions, though of an earlier phase. The Pāṇḍiyas appear to have issued punch-marked coins in both silver and copper (*Figure 2.3*).

The Shaṅgam texts have much to say about the Choḷa rulers

FIGURE 2.3 Punch-marked Pāṇḍiyan coinage in silver and copper. P.L. Gupta.

and princes, who are not represented either by coins or inscriptions. Karikāla (*c.* AD 190) is said to have defeated both his Chera and Pāṇḍiya contemporaries in a single battle. As to the Satiyaputa chief mentioned in the Jambai inscription, Atiyan Neṭumān Añchi, he is celebrated as a great warrior chief in Shaṅgam literature. He is said to have been ultimately overthrown by the Chera ruler Peruñcheral Irampurai.

The Shaṅgam texts give us a picture of monarchical states with no hint anywhere of tribal polities. The ruler's patronage was the biggest source of individuals' income and wealth; and the quality that was most praised in the ruler by the bards was military prowess. The army comprised chariots, elephants, cavalry and infantry; and martial traditions glorified war and death. The suicide of widows on the death of the fallen ruler or warrior – the dreaded practice of 'sati' – was now commonly demanded by courtly ethics.

Of taxes we learn little. That a king should bring water to land is urged at one place. An inscription of second century BC records a tank built by villagers. Whether this implies the existence of a village community or assembly is, however, doubtful. Shaṅgam poets sometimes express anxiety about murder and robbery on the routes, and assume it to be a kingly obligation to suppress them.

TABLE 2.1 Chronology (all dates approximate)

	BC
Choḷas and Pāṇḍiyas, major states in south India	258
Beginning of period of Tamil-Brāhmī inscriptions	200
Pushyamitra established Shuṅga dynasty	185
Grammarian Patañjali flourished	150
Bhāgabhadra/Bhāgavata, Shuṅga ruler of Vidisha reigned	115–83
Rise of the Sātavāhana dynasty	100
Khāravela, ruler of Kaliṅga: his Hathigumpha inscription	20
	AD
Period of the Shaṅgam (Chankam) texts	1–300
Gotamīputa Sātakani, Sātavāhana king	100
Pulumāvi, successor to preceding	130
Vāsishṭhī Sātakarṇi, defeated by Rudradāman	145
Karikāla, Choḷa ruler	190
End of the Sātavāhana dynasty	200

Extract 2.1
Post-Mauryan Dynastic History, according to the *Purāṇas*

Shuṅgas

Pushyamitra, the commander-in-chief (*senānīr*), will uproot Brihadratha the last Mauryan king and will rule the kingdom as king 36 years. His son Agnimitra will be king 8 years. Vasujyeshtha will be king 7 years. His son Vasumitra will be king 10 years. Then his son Andhraka will reign 2 years. Pulindaka will then reign 8 years. His son Ghosha will be king 3 years. Next, Vajramitra will be king 9 years. Bhāgavata will be king 32 years. His son Devabhūmi will reign 10 years.

These 10 Shuṅga kings will enjoy this earth full 112 years. From them the earth will pass to the Kāṇvas. . . .

Andhras

The Andhra Simuka [in the originals: Shishuka, Sindhuka, Shipraka] with his fellow-tribesmen, the servants of Susharman [the last Kāṇva ruler] will assail the Kāṇvāyanas and him (Susharman), and destroy the remains of the Shuṅgas' power and will obtain this earth. Simuka will be king 23 years. His younger brother Krishṇa will reign 10 years. His son Shrī Shātakarṇi will reign 10 years. Then Pūrnotsaṇga will be king 18 years. Skandhastambhi will be king 18 yers. Shātakarṇi will reign 56 years, his son Lambodara 18 years. His son Āpīlaka will reign 12 years. Meghasvāti will reign 18 years. Svāti will be king 18 years. Skandasvāti will be king 7 years. Mrigendra Svātikarṇa will reign 3 years. Kuntala Svātikarṇa will be king 8 years. Svātikarṇa will be king one year. Pulomāvi will reign 36 years. Arishṭakarṇa will reign 25 years. Then Hāla will be king 5 years. Mantalaka will be a powerful king 5 years. Purikashеṇa will reign 21 years. Sundara Shātakarṇi will reign one year. Chakora Shātakarṇi will reign 6 months. Shivasvāti will reign 28 years. King Gautamīputra will be king next 21 years. His son Pulomā will reign 28 years. (Shātakarṇi will be king 29 years – doubtful insertion in one version.) Shivashrī Puloma will be king 7 years. His son Shivaskandha Shātakarṇi will be king three (?) years. Yajñashrī Shātakarṇika will reign 29 [var. 19] years. After him Vijaya will be king 6 years. His son Chaṇḍashrī Shātakarṇi will reign 10 years. Another of them Pulomāvi will reign 7 years.

These 30 Andhra kings will enjoy the earth 460 years.

F.E. Pargiter's translation in his *Purāṇa Text of the Dynasties of the Kali Age,* London, 1913, pp. 70–72.

Extract 2.2
The Hathigumpha Inscription of Khāravela, Orissa, first century BC (Prakrit)

Salutation to the *arahaṁtas* [Jinas]! Salutation to all *siḍhas*. The noble *mahārāja* Mahāmeghavāhana, scion of the Cheti royal dynasty with excellent and auspicious marks and features, possessed of virtues which have spread over the four quarters, the Kaliṁga-sovereign (*Kaliṁgādhipati*), the illustrious Khāravela, endowed with a body, ruddy and handsome, having spent fifteen years in youthful sport and in fully learning writing (*lekha*), painting (*rūpa*), arithmetic (*gaṇana*), business (*vavahāra*) and law (*vidhi*), he remained crown-prince (*yovaraja*) for nine years.

After attaining full twenty-five years, prosperous since infancy, destined to bẹ as ever victorious as Venā, he was crowned as *mahārāja* in the third Kaliṁga royal dynasty.

In the first year, soon after the coronation, he repaired the storm-battered gate-towers, enclosing walls and buildings in Kalimganagara; he caused the erection of embankments of the lake (*tala*), Khibīra-isi, and of tanks and cisterns and the restoration of gardens; done at the cost of thirty-five hundred thousand to gratify his subjects.

In the second year, ignoring Sātakamni he sent westward his army, strong in cavalry, elephants, infantry and chariots; and the army destroyed the city of Asika on the banks of the Kañhabeṁṇa.

In the third year, he, being versed in science of music (*gaṁdhava-veda-budho*), entertained the City (*nagara*) with *dapa* (?) performances, dancing, singing, instrumental music and by holding festivities and assemblies (*samāja*).

In the fourth year at Vijādharā what was built by the past rulers of Kalimga not damaged before . . . having been shorn of their coronets and helmets (?) and with their umbrellas and *bhiṅgaras* (?) cast away, deprived of their jewels, all the Raṭhikas and Bhojakas were made to bow down at his feet.

In the fifth year, what the Nanda Rāja had laid out three hundred years ago (*ti-vasa-sata*, also rendered: 103 years), he brought from Tansuliya a canal (*paṇādi*) to the City (*nagara*).

In the sixth year, in the course of performing *rājasūya*, he remitted all taxes (*kara*) and cesses (*vaṇa*) and bestowed privileges, (worth) hundred thousands, to the various castes (*jāti*) of *porajānapada* (= Sanskrit: *paurajānapada*).

In the seventh year . . . Vajiraghara . . .

In the eighth year, with a large army . . . after sacking Goradhagira he devastated Rājagaha. From report of this success, to save his army (*sena*) and carriages (*vahana)*, Dimita (?), the Yavana *rāja*, retreated to Madhura. . . . He gave away *kapa* trees, elephants, chariots with their drivers, houses, residences, rest-houses, and gave [tax-] exemptions to Brahmaṇas on his triumphal return.

Arahata . . .

[In the ninth year] . . . he built a big palace Mahāvijaya at the cost of thirty-eight hundred thousand.

In the tenth year . . . pursuing the policy of chastisement (*daṁḍa*) and alliance (*saṁdhī*) and conciliation (?), he set out to conquer Bharadhavasa (= Sanskrit: Bhāratavarsha) . . .

[In the eleventh year], he obtained riches made of jewels and precious things . . . Built by a previous ruler, Pīthuṁḍa he ploughed up by asses; and (he) broke up the 1300-year old Tramira [Dravida or Tamil] country-union (*daha-saṁghātaṁ*) that posed a danger to the *janapada*.

In the twelfth year he terrified the *rājas* of Utarāpadha (Sanskrit:

Uttarāpatha) . . . with thousands of . . . Creating fear among the Māgadhas, he made them drive their elephants into the Gaṅgā. He made the Māgadha *rāja* Bahasatimita bow at his feet. He set up (the image of) the Kaliṁga Jina which had been taken away by Naṁda *rāja* . . . and caused to be brought home the wealth (*vasu*) of Aṁga-Magadha, along with the keepers of the family jewels of (?) . . . He built . . . excellent towers with carved interiors and settled hundreds of masons with tax-remissions (?). He raised a marvellous stockade for driving in elephants . . . and horses, elephants, jewels and rubies, as well as numerous pearls he caused to be brought here from the Paṁḍa [Pāṇḍiya] *rāja* . . . he subjugates.

In the thirteenth year on the Kumārā Hill, where the wheel of conquest [by Jina] has been well revolved, he offered respectfully China cloth (*china-vatāni*) [silks] and white clothes to *arahats*, who have extinguished the cycle of lives, the preachers on the religious life and conduct at the Relic Memorial. By the illustrious Khāravela, a lay-worshipper [himself], was realized the [nature of] soul and body . . . Bringing about an assemblage of wise ascetics and sages from a hundred quarters, the *samaṇas* (monks) of good deeds and conforming [with injunctions] . . . near the Relic Repository of the Arahat on the top of the hill . . . with stones . . . brought from many *yojanas* (leagues), quarried from excellent mines . . . He set up four columns inlaid with beryl . . . at the cost of seventy-five hundred thousand; he caused to be completed expeditiously the seven-fold *Aṁgas* of the sixty-four letters. King of peace, king of prosperity, king of monks (*bhikhu*), King of *Dhama* [*Dharma*], who has been seeing, hearing and realizing blessings . . . Accomplished in extraordinary virtues, respecter of all sects (*sava-pāsaṁḍa-pūjako*), the repairer of all temples (*devāya*), one whose army and chariots are invincible, whose dominions are protected by their head (himself), descended from the family of the royal sage Vasu, the great conqueror, the *rāja*, the illustrious Khāravela.

Note: In the original text of the inscription, the present tense is used throughout for all the past events and the deeds of Khāravela. This is altered in the above rendering to the past tense. Owing to the fact that the rock-face is much worn out, there has been much controversy over readings of portions of this inscription. We have, with some caution, drawn on the K.P. Jayaswal and R.D. Banerji translation, published in *Epigraphia Indica*, XX, pp. 71–89, and have checked it with the text as deciphered by D.C. Sircar, *Select Inscriptions, Bearing on Indian History and Civilization*, Vol. I, second edition, Calcutta, 1965, No. 91 (= Krishnan, No. 67).

Extract 2.3

Siri-Puḷumāyi Vasiṭhiputa Sātakaṇi's Eulogy of Gotamīputa Sātakaṇi, Nasik Cave Inscription, *c.* AD 160 (Prakrit)

Success! In the nineteenth – 19th-year of *raño* (king) Siri-Pulumāyi Vāsiṭhīputa, in the second – 2nd – fortnight of summer, on the thirteenth – 13th – day: The king of kings (*rāja-raño*) Gotamīputa, who was in strength equal to the Himavata, Meru and Madara mountains, the *rāja* of Asika, Asaka, Muḷaka, Suraṭha, Kukura, Aparaṁta, Anupa, Vidhaba, (and) Ākara-Avati, lord over the moutains of Vijha, Chhavata, Pārichāta, Sahya, Kaṇhagiri, Macha, Siriṭana, Malaya, Mahida, Seṭagiri (and) Chakora; obeyed by the circle of all kings (*rājas*) on earth; whose face was beautiful and pure like the lotus opened by the rays of the sun . . . [praises of his person follow, that are here omitted]; of unchecked obedience towards his mother; who properly devised time and place for the pursuit of the triple object (of human activity); who sympathized with the weal and woe of townsmen-and-people (*porajanani*); who crushed the pride and conceit of the Khatiyas (K<u>sh</u>atriyas), who destroyed the Saka, Yavana and Palhava; who never levied or employed taxes (*kara*), but in conformity with justice (*dhama*); alien to hurting life even towards an offending enemy; the furtherer of the homesteads of the twice-born (*dijāvara*) and the lowly (*kuṭuba*); who rooted out the Khakharāta race (*vasa*); who restored the glory of the Sātavāhana family (*kula*); whose feet were saluted by all provinces (*maḍala*); who stopped the admixture of the four *vaṇas* (Sanskrit: *varṇas*); who conquered multitudes of enemies in many battles . . . [further praises of his personal attainments follow that are here omitted]; the unique Brāhmaṇa (*eka-bamhaṇa*); in prowess equal to Rāma, Kesava, Arjuna, Bhīmasena; liberal on festive days in unceasing festivities and assemblies; not inferior in lustre to Nābhāga, Nahusa, Janamejaya, Sakara [Sagara], Yayāti, Rāma, Abarīsa [Ambarī<u>sh</u>a]; . . . [further praises, omitted], who raised his family (*kula*) to high fortune.

Siri Sātakaṇi [Gotamīputa]'s mother, the great queen (*mahādevī*), Gotami Balasirī, delighting in truth, charity, patience and respect for life; bent on penance, self-control, restraint and abstinence, fully having the bearing of the wife of a royal sage (*rāja-risi*) caused as a pious gift on the top of the Tiraṇhu mountain similar to the top of Kailāsa, this cave to be made quite equal to the divine mansions. And that cave the great queen, mother of a *mahārāja* and grandmother of a *mahārāja*, gives to the Sagha (*Sangha*) of Bhikhus (monks) in the person of the fraternity of the Bhadāyanīyas; and for the sake of embellishment of that cave, with a view to honouring and pleasing the great queen, his grandmother, his grandson [Vāsiṭhīputa] . . . lord of

[Dakhiṇa-]patha, making over the merit of the gift to his father, grants to this meritorious donation, the village of Pisājipadaka on the south-west side of Tiraṇhu mountain. Renunciation of enjoyments of every kind!

Note: The translation is based mainly on the reading and rendering of E. Senart, *Epigraphia Indica*, VIII, pp. 60–65, with a shift of the passage relating to the 'great queen' to the position it has in the arrangement of contents of the original inscription.

Note 2.1
The Purāṇas

Purāṇa, as an adjective, means 'old, ancient'; but already in the *Atharvaveda*, datable to *c.* 800 BC, the word is used for 'ancient lore', which, of course, would mean the story of the past as narrated according to popular or priests' belief and so would include an extending mass of mythology. What are known as *Purāṇas*, conventionally held to be eighteen in number, are texts that contain much detail about Brāhmaṇa ritual, along with statements about what has happened in our present evil age, the *Kali-yuga*, which began after the Bhārata war. These texts have continued to be embellished, altered, added to and expanded down the ages, so that the same *Purāṇa* could exist in many versions. Scholars have diligently distinguished the earlier texts, mainly by the device of picking those versions whose *Kali-yuga* annals end at the earliest point. F.E. Pargiter, in 1913, published an annotated edition and translation of such early versions, though even in these the language, forms of names, orders of sequence of rulers, etc., vary considerably. The texts edited by Pargiter, despite the discovery of other manuscripts and versions, seem still to be the best representatives of the earliest stratum in this body of quasi-historical literature.

The *Purāṇas*, in their annals, consist mainly of rulers' names with the numbers of years to which their reigns extended. The form taken is that of prediction made by Suta (or by Parāshara) at the beginning of the Kali age as to what is going to happen in future. Thus the past (*purāṇa*) is presented as the future (*bhavishya*); and there is actually a *Bhavishya Purāṇa* (now with much alloyed text), which a set of other early *Purāṇas* acknowledge to be the source they draw on. Since the skeletal dynastic accounts omit any account of the Gupta dynasty, except for a bare passing reference, it is believed that the early *Purāṇa* texts were composed around the beginning of the fourth century AD. The metrical portions and many names, notably in the annals of the dynasties from the time of Gautama Buddha onwards, suggest that their sources lay in earlier compilations of Prakrit ballads and popular enumerations of rulers, which were then put into Sanskrit. In other words, while the source of the pre-Buddha dynasties was probably a construction of Brahmanical tradition, the annals of the Shishunāga dynasty of Magadha and subsequent dynasties had possibly more popular Prakrit sources.

It is likely that in these Purāṇic annals, the historical portion begins only with the Shishunāga dynasty. From here onwards we are able to verify parts at least of the Purāṇic lists from other sources. Vimbisāra (Bimbisāra) and Ajatashatru of the Shishunāga dynasty appear in Buddhist annals of the life of Gautama Buddha. Of the Mauryas, the Purāṇic annals of at least the first three rulers similarly accord with Buddhist annals, and, otherwise too, with what the Greek accounts and Ashoka's inscriptions tell us. While, therefore, caution is to be exercised in making use of Purāṇic dynastic lists (their order of sequence, reign periods, even names of individual rulers may not be in many cases reliable or accurate), these still constitute a valuable source for us. As in the case of Mauryan times, these can be verified on certain points by reference to inscriptions; and this again shows that their evidence is not to be summarily dismissed. It may be seen from our present chapter that in view of the scantiness of information to be gained from inscriptions and coins for the indigenous dynasties from *c.* 200 BC to AD 100, the *Purāṇas* alone offer, in the case of at least three dynasties (the Shuṅgas, Kāṇvāyanas and Andhras), a passable framework of dynastic history, which may then be verified or modified by reference to other evidence.

Note 2.2
Shaṅgam Texts

Shaṅgam (also spelt Chankam) texts form the earliest body of Tamil literature. The term *shaṅgam* means an assemblage or 'academy' where literary compositions, especially poems, were recited and judged. Tradition speaks of three such successive *shaṅgams*, which extended, in all, to over 9,990 years! Both historical and literary criticism has led to the view that *shaṅgam* poems were composed and circulated in an early period, to be much later put into anthologies. These anthologies are eight in number, called *Togai* or *Eṭṭut-togai,* and coexist with ten long poems, grouped in a set called *Pāṭṭu* or *Pattup-pāṭṭu*. These had assumed their present form by the fourteenth century, and thus contain compositions spread over a long period. The earlier portion, to which historians now apply the designation of *Shaṅgam*, has been reduced to over 2,000 poems found in six anthologies and a collection of longer poems. In themes, these poems range from those of love to paeans addressed to gods, and of exploits of war to eulogies of rulers. The strong influence of Brahmanical ritual and divinities, and infusion of Prakrit and Sanskrit vocabulary suggest a post-Muaryan date for even the earliest Shaṅgam compositions. From references to Yavanas coming on their vessels to carry on trade, it has been deduced that they belong to the period of the flourishing Roman trade of the early centuries AD. Similarly, from the late tradition attesting to the Chera ruler Shenguṭṭavan, mentioned in the Shaṅgam texts, as ruling contemporaneously with the Sri Lankan ruler Gajabāhu, datable from the Sinhalese chronicle, *Mahāvamsa*, to the late second century AD, an important chronological 'synchronism' has been inferred, enabling Shenguṭṭavan to be also placed in the second century. On the basis of such evidence, the Shaṅgam compositions have been held to belong to the first three centuries of the Christian era.

Shaṅgam literature constitutes an undoubtedly rich source of the history of Tamil Nadu. In respect of beliefs, social customs, rituals, etc., its importance is manifest. For political history too, in view of the meagre information to be derived from Tamil-Brāhmī inscriptions, the poems have been sought to be used as a massive quarry. The excessive exaggeration, inflated eulogies and claims of impossible achievements credited to the poets' heroes must, however, all be heavily discounted, before the contours of even dynasties and their conflicts can be worked out, or the nature of polities of the time discerned, with any amount of clarity. Nonetheless, the residue that remains is still of great value to the historian.

Note 2.3

Bibliographical Note

Among general works covering the dynasties mentioned in this chapter, the most detailed is K.A. Nilakantha Sastri (ed.), *A Comprehensive History of India*, Vol. II: *The Mauryas and Sātavāhanas, 325 BC – AD 300*, Bombay, 1957; it is still serviceable, especially its chapters IV, V, X for northern India and the Deccan, and chapters XVI and XVII for south India. Chapter XXI contains a critical account of Shaṅgam literature. On the Sātavāhanas, the major recent work is Ajay Mitra Shastri's *The Sātavāhanas and the Western Kshatrapas*, Nagpur, 1998. In Patrick Olivelle (ed.), *Between the Two Empires: Society in India, 300 BCE to 400 CE*, Indian edition, New Delhi, 2007, chapters 4 (S. Bhandare) and 6 (H. Falk) engage with political history.

As for sources, an extensive collection of the Prakrit and Sanskrit inscriptions of the period has been compiled by K.G. Krishnan in his *Prakrit and Sanskrit Epigraphs*, mentioned already in *Note 1.2*. The classic work on Tamil-Brāhmī inscriptions is Iravatham Mahadevan, *Early Tamil Epigraphy, From the Earliest Times to the Sixth Century AD*, Chennai, 2003; it contains a very detailed introduction. Romila Thapar, *The Past Before Us: Historical Tradition of Early North India*, Ranikhet, 2013, has a chapter (pp. 265–318) on the *Purāṇas*.

3
The Kushān Empire

3.1 Origins of Kushān Power

We have seen in *Chapter 1.1* that Bactria (northern Afghanistan) under Greek rule was under pressure from nomadic tribes settled north of the Oxus as early as 208–06 BC. The prosperous Greek city of Ai Khanum, on the north-eastern corner of Bactria, possibly fell to them by 145 BC. By 50 BC, Greek rule in Bactria as a whole appears to have been brought to an end.

For the nomadic movements in Central Asia beyond Bactria, we have evidence from quite early Chinese sources. The famous historian Szuma Chien (Sima Qian), in his *Shih-chi* ('Historical Records') written *c.* 100 BC, tells us of a large tribe called **Yueh-chi** (Yue-zhi) which, in the third and second centuries BC, was evicted from its original home in Western Gansu (northern China) and forced to move across Xinjiang (western China) under pressure from the Hiung-nu nomads.

By the last quarter of the second century, the Yueh-chi, possessed of 100,000 to 200,000 bowmen, had entered 'Ta-hia' and established themselves north of the Oxus river. It is generally agreed that 'Ta-hia' is the Chinese transcription of Tokhara, which name seems to have been first applied to Trans-oxiana. That region, previous to the Yueh-chi occupation, was divided into a number of principalities, whose people, according to Szuma Chien, were weak in warfare though adept in commerce. Since a part of the Yueh-chi had been left behind in Xinjiang, the Yueh-chi in Tahia came to be called the Great ('Ta') Yueh-chi by the Chinese, to distinguish them from their fellow tribesmen, the Little Yueh-chi, who had stayed back.

Subsequently, according to Greek accounts, Bactria was

overrun by the Asioi, Pasianoi, the Tocharoi and the Sacarauloi (Strabo, XI.8.2). Strabo himself elsewhere (XI.8.4) refers to Bactria being conquered by the Sakai or Sakas, who might also be represented by the name 'Sacarauloi' in his first statement. As we have seen, the final supplanting of Greek rule in Bactria had taken place by 50 BC. In this, besides the Sakas, the Yueh-chi might have also had a hand, being represented by the 'Tocharoi' (Tokharans), who are named among the invaders by Strabo, as we have just seen.

The next instalment of information about the Yueh-chi in Chinese sources is contained in the 'History of the Han Dynasty' (*Han Shu*) by Pan Gu (d. AD 92). 'Ta-hia' now meant Bactria, which had passed completely in the hands of the Great Yueh-chi. It contained under them five principalities (*hi-hou*), one of which was that of Kuei-shang with its capital at Hu-tsao. In Kuei-shang, as a territory and, perhaps, also a tribal settlement, one can discern the first mention of **Kushān**, the name of the great future dynasty. At the same time it is clear that, at least till the first part of the first century AD, the Kushāns had not gained much power in their homeland of Bactria and were subservient to the Great Yueh-chi.

A sensational find, that of the graves at Tilla (or Tillya) Tepe, yielding over 20,000 gold objects of local craftsmanship that display influences of both Hellenistic and Central Asian craft traditions, can be dated to the first part of the first century AD by the find of a gold coin of the Roman emperor Tiberius (reigned, AD 14–37). Among the many astonishing features of this site is that, amidst all its wealth, it is wholly non-literate. No local writing whatever could be discovered on any object or stone. There is no contemporary local coinage either. The enormous amount of worked gold certainly suggests that the ruling class must have obtained a massive share of the surplus out of the local produce, which it could convert into precious metal through trade channels and services of skilled craftsmen. Such conditions of aristocratic or royal wealth are also indicated by the excavations at Begram, north of Kabul, on a strategically placed pass in the Hindu-kush. Here were unearthed store-rooms containing Roman artefacts of first century AD, alongside Chinese lacquerware of late first century BC and early first century AD.

It is likely that at some stage, later in the first century AD, a major political change took place and the Kushāns, from being sub-rulers of a part, obtained dominance over the whole of Bactria. We have here to turn again to the Chinese annals, our specific source being the 'History of the Late Han Dyansty', *Hou Han-shu,* compiled by Fan Ye (AD 445). Drawing upon the report sent to the Chinese court by Pan Yang (Bao Yong), *c.* AD 127, we are told of the Kushāns, who were now masters of Bactria and other territories, that 'in all the [surrounding] kingdoms they are spoken of as "King of Kuei-shuang [Kushān]", but the Han [emperors of China] stuck to their old designation and called them Ta (the Great) Yueh-chi'. It is thus not clear whether the Kushān rulers really sprang from the Yueh-chi stock at all, or whether they were simply called Yueh-chi by the Chinese court because they ruled the area of which previously the Yueh-chi had been in possession. What we know for certain is that when, under the Kushāns, Bactria turned literate again, it turned to an essentially Iranian dialect – written in Greek script – which historians now call 'Bactrian', but which to its speakers was known simply as 'Aria' or Iranian (see *Extract 3.1*). If the Yueh-chi had spoken any other language and the Kushāns were really descendants of the Yueh-chi, both the language as well as the ethnic affiliation had now been long forgotten. They held themselves to be, and spoke the language of, Arias or Iranians.

3.2 Early History of the Kushān Dynasty

The Rabatak inscription from Bactria (north Afghanistan), discovered in 1993 (*Extract 3.1*), has finally established what historians had long deduced from other evidence, that the founder of Kushān power and the originator of the line of Kushān emperors was **Kajula Kadphises** (or Kadphises I), though his name is spelt as Kozala Kadaphis (Greek letters) and Kajula Kasa or Kaphasa (Kharoshṭhī) on his coins, and Kozoulo Kadphiso in the Rabatak inscription. He calls himself Kushana in his coins. He is referred to as the chief (*hi-hou*) of 'Kuei-shuang', called 'Kiu-tsiu-kio' (Que-jiu-que) in the report of *c.* 127 in the *Hou Han-shu*. He is there reported to have subjugated all the other four principalities of Ta-hia (Bactria), and then to have seized Kao-fu (Kabul) and Kipin (Kashmir). His foray to the south of the Hindukush mountains could have happened only after the Parthian ruler Gondophares's Takht-i Bāhī (NWFP) inscription of year 103 of the

Azes era (date within possible range of AD 73–111). But if, as the speculation goes, he is the *erjhina* (prince) Kapa mentioned in that inscription, he might have already obtained some important position as an ally or nominal subordinate of the Parthian ruler. In any case, by year 122 (presumably of the Azes era), a reigning *maharaya* Gushana is mentioned in an inscription from Panjtar (NWFP); and by the year 136, expressly of the Azes era, a Kushān emperor, with the usual titles henceforth used by the line (*maharaja rajatiraja devaputra*), finds place in the Taxila silver scroll. These two inscriptions suggest that some time, possibly by AD 92 (taking the epoch of the Azes era to be placed in the range of 30 BC – AD 8), Kajula Kadphises had taken possession of the region of Gandhāra. That he also held Swat valley is shown by the inscription from Odi (Swat, NWFP), whose local ruler Senavarma acknowledges the suzerainty of *maharaja rayatiraya* Kuyula Kataphsa and honours his son, the *devaputra* Sadaṉhkaṇa. Kadphises I's occupation of Kipin or Kashmir is evidenced by his successor Vima Kadphises's inscription at Khalatse in Ladakh (Jammu & Kashmir). Chinese annals tell us of a raid in AD 90 led by a Yueh-chi general (*sahi*) across the Pamirs into Xin Jiang, which the Chinese forces under Pan Cha'o were able to repel. This could have been an expedition sent by Kajula Kadphises from Kashmir.

According to the *Hou Han-shu*, Kajula Kadphises (Kiu-tsui-kio) died at the age of 80 years and was succeeded by his son Yen-kao-chen (Yen Gao-zhen), whom it has been usual to identify with **Vima Kadphises** of the coins. However, by one reading (by Sims-Williams) of the Rabatak inscription, Kajula Kadphises's son's name was Vima Taktoo, the *shao* (*shāh*), not otherwise known, whose son and successor, in turn, was Vima ('Ooema') Kadphisa. B.N. Mukherjee has read the whole line differently and seen here a reference to 'Saddashkana', the son of Kajula mentioned in the Odi inscription. He also does not read the word *sha* (king) for him, so that Sadaṉhkaṇa would not seem to have succeeded his father as ruler, it being his son Vima Kadphises who actually became the king upon Kajula Kadphises's death, though he was his grandson and not, contrary to the *Hou Han-shu*, his son.

In the Rabatak inscription Vima Kadphises's second name is the same as that of Kajula Kadphises (in the form 'Kadphisa'); and this is also borne out by the legends on this ruler's coins. As for the variant 'Ooema Takpiso', this appears in the Bactrian text of the trilingual Dasht-i Nawar inscription, while the Kharoshṭhī text has 'Vhama Kusa', and the version in the third language, according to Harmatta, has 'Katvisa'. This suggests that Takpiso was a Bactrian variant of Vima Kadphises's second name; it is found also in the Dilbarjin and Surkh Kotal inscriptions in Bactria. Since the *Hou Han-shu*, in which Vima Kadphises is mentioned as Yen-chen, depended on a report submitted to the Chinese court about AD 127, he should have come to the throne before that time. In Bactria and its neighbourhood his inscriptions use a Bactrian era of an unknown epoch: the Dasht-i Nawar inscription bears the year 279, while Surkh Kotal has 299. These dates show that his reign must have lasted longer than twenty years. His Khalatse inscription is presumably dated in the Azes era, which prevailed outside Bactria: its date, the year 184 or 187, cannot be placed earlier than AD 154 or 157.

According to the *Hou Han-shu*, Sind ('T'ienchu, also called Shen-tu') had now been conquered by the Kushāns; its king had been killed and a Kushān ('Yueh-chi') governor had been installed in his place. It is possible that Vima Kadphises also overthrew the Saka regime at Mathura, if it had survived up to his time. A label on a colossal statue at Mat near Mathura bears the name Vima Takshuma, with the added designation of Kushanaputra. The statue was apparently set up at a 'god-house' (*devakula*) built by an officer (*bakanapati*) of the king. As we shall see, it becomes clear from the Rabatak inscription that the Kushān emperors were now trying to place themselves among the divinities, for similar 'god-houses' were constructed in Bactria as well (see *Chapter 3.5* below).

Vima Kadphises's reign marks important cultural and administrative developments. His Bactrian inscriptions at Dasht-i Nawar, Dilbarjin and Surkh Kotal show that the local Iranian dialect written in Greek script was now the official language of the area. A second remarkable change that comes with Vima Kadphises is in coinage. Kajula Kadphises merely issued copper coins, copying Indo-Greek models, to the extent of imitating the Indo-Greek ruler Hermaeus so far as to use his bust and legend on the obverse (*Figure 3.1:1*). Vima Kadphises created practically a new coinage, minting gold, for which

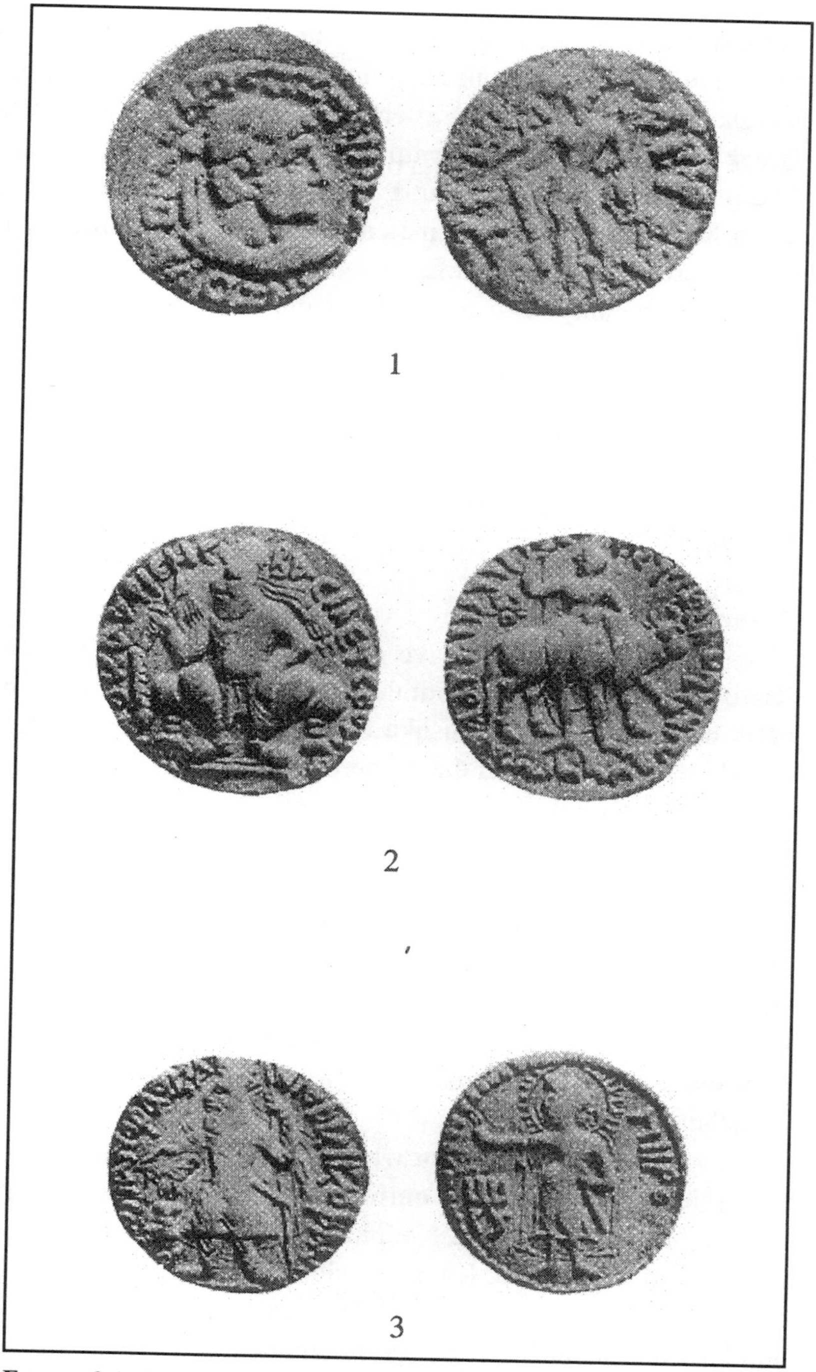

FIGURE 3.1 (1) Hermaeus–Kajula Kadphises copper coin; (2) Gold coin of Vima Kadphises; (3) Gold coin of Kaṇishka. R.B. Whitehead.

there was no precedent in even Bactrian Greek coinage after its earliest phase (*Figure 3.1:2*). Both his gold and copper coins followed Roman weights (those established after Nero's reform of AD 64), and bore Greek legends (no longer corrupt) as well as Kharoshṭhī on the reverse. The new coins had propaganda value too: in some of his gold issues Vima Kadphises appears depicted as god Mithras ('Miiro') with sun-rays radiating from his head.

Probably with his Indian subjects in view, Vima Kadphises depicted Lord Shiva with his trident on the reverse of his coins, whereas his father's coins had mainly contained representations of Herakles. Indeed, Vima Kadphises even sought to induct Shiva among Bactria's official divinities. At Dilbarjin, a wall-painting of Shiva and Pārvati has been found in a 'god-house' which contains an inscription of Vima Kadphises.

3.3 Kaṇishka

For reasons we have given in our *Note 3.1*, we have placed Kaṇishka's accession at about the year AD 160. While it had been quite early determined that Kaṇishka could not have preceded Kadphises I and II but had succeeded them, there was some doubt, due mainly to an abandonment of the Kharoshṭhī legends on his coins, as to whether Kaṇishka actually belonged to his predecessors' line. There were strong suggestions made, as by Sten Konow in his standard collection of Kharoshṭhī inscriptions, that Kaṇishka belonged to the Little Yueh-chi, had come from Khotan and supplanted the earlier Kushān dynasty. All such speculations have been laid to rest by Kaṇishka's own Rabatak inscription, which shows that he was the son and immediate successor of Vima Kadphises, and that, like him, Bactria and not Khotan was his homeland.

The inscription (for which see *Extract 3.1*) makes it clear that Kaṇishka inherited a **large empire**, extending deep into India. While, as we have seen, Vima Kadphises had already conquered Indian territory up to Mathura, Kaṇishka claims that he had enlarged it further by conquering Ujjain, Sāketa (Ayodhya), Kausambi (near Allahabad) and Pāṭaliputra, and 'as far as Shri-Champa' (the last in district Bhagal-pur, Bihar). Since the Rabatak inscription was set up in his very 1st regnal year (which also became the initial year of the Kushān era), the conquests he here specifies must have been made by him during the late years of his father's reign. That this was no idle boast on his part is shown by the geographical spread of the inscriptions recognizing him as emperor. Such inscriptions have been found at Kausambi (of year 2); Sarnath near Varanasi ('Bārānasi') (of year 3), further east; and Shravasti ('Shāvasti') (with date lost), north of Ayodhya. At Sanchi, in the year 22, there is an inscription which gives the sovereign's name as 'Vas-kuṣhāṇa', indicating, despite the puzzle posed by the name, that the area of Vidisha was now under Kushān control, even if no such direct evidence is available for Ujjain.

In the north Kaṇiṣhka maintained Kushān authority up to the shadows of the Pamirs, as is indicated by his Hunza rock inscription. There may, then, be a grain of truth in the late story, recorded by Yuan Chwang (*c.* 640), that he even received some princely hostages from western China, whom he kept at Chīna-bhukti in the Panjab.

While the importance he attached to the Indian possessions is shown by the repeated references to India in the Rabatak inscription, it seems from it that Kaṇiṣhka at his accession also made a special effort to keep and deepen the sense of loyalty to his dynasty in the Bactrian homeland. It was proclaimed that the 'Aria' (Bactrian) language was now to replace Greek. On his coins the Greek letters not only replace Kharoṣhṭhī characters altogether, but in time carry the Bactrian rather than Greek forms of names and words (*Figure 3.1:3*).

In Bactria he followed a **religious policy** extolling local deities. On the reverse sides of his coins he first depicted Greek deities, Helios, Hephaistos and Salene, but then shifted to representations of the Iranian divine figures popular in Bactria, such as Nana, a goddess of Near Eastern origin, and the Iranian gods Meiro (Mithras), Athro (fire god) and Mao (moon god). For his Indian subjects, there are representations of 'Okro' (Shiva) and 'Boddo' (the Buddha). But in the Rabatak inscription the deities are all those worshipped in Bactria, Umma/Nana, and the Iranian, especially Zoroastrian deities including Ahura Mazda (God proper), and two possibly Sogdian gods, with only two deities supplied with Indian names, Mahasena and Vishakha. Shiva and the Buddha are not mentioned.

Kaṇiṣhka had images made at Rabatak of the deities for a 'god-house' (*bagolango*, a word often mistranslated as 'sanctuary'). The worship of gods was to be accompanied with the worship of the kings of his dynasty, from his great-grandfather down to himself, all represented in three-dimensional images. The kings were 'sons of god' (in Bactrian, *bogapoor*; in Prakrit and Sanskrit, *devaputra*), and so deities themselves. Clearly, the device was being employed to claim for them a further entitlement to loyalty from their Bactrian subjects. Kaṇishka built yet another 'god-house' at Surkh-kotal, where a Bactrian inscription tells us that the temple was begun in Kaṇishka's first year and completed in year 31 (under Huvishka). Its designation 'Bagolango' survives in the modern geographical name Baghlan. As we have seen, a similar 'god-house' (*devakula*) had been built at Mat near Mathura under Vima Kadphises; a famous statue of Kaṇishka (so spelt), named in the label-inscription on the lower part of the statue, was now installed there (*Figure 3.2*). It is possible that the claims to divinity already implied in the Odi inscription, where Kajula Kadphises's son Sadashkaṇa is described as a *devaputra*, derived partly from foreign precedents: some of the Seleucids had proclaimed their divinity and so did the Caesars of Rome. The latter's coinage exercised great influence on Kushān coinage from Vima Kadphises's time onwards, and 'kaisara' (= caesar) occurs as one of the titles of the Kushān emperor in the Ara inscription of the year 41. The usefulness of such a claim to impose loyalty upon all subjects was however so manifest that Vima Kadphises had already made his coins add to his titles the Prakrit phrase *sarvalogo ishvara*, 'Lord/God of all people'; and Kaṇishka was thus merely continuing and reinforcing an established tradition.

In Bactria, as we have seen, Kaṇishka does not seem to have shown any particular regard for the Buddha or Buddhism. In his Indian possessions, however, greater attention needed to be paid to that religion. It was noted in the Chinese report of *c.* AD 127 incorporated in the *Hou Han-shu*, that in Shen-tu (Sind), 'the inhabitants . . . practise the religion of the Buddha.' The Buddha began to be depicted on Kaṇishka's coins at par with other deities, as we have seen. There is the inscription of year 11 at Sui Vihar, a ruined *stupa* near Bahawalpur (southern Panjab, Pakistan), where the name of the sovereign, *maharaja rajatiraja Devaputra* Kaṇishka, is recorded; and a Buddhist nun and monk mention Kaṇishka's name in their inscriptions while visiting Kausambi, Sarnath and Shravasti. One inscription (the

FIGURE 3.2 Kaṇishka statue at Mat, near Mathura. UNESCO.

'Peshawar casket' from Shahjiki Dheri, of year 1) records his construction of a Buddhist structure, namely the 'Kaṇishka *vihāra*'; otherwise, there is no record of any donation to Buddhist monasteries or monks, except for a doubtful general reference to Kaṇishka making a donation (*dana*) to the Buddhist Sangha, found in a graffito on Hunza rock near the Pamirs.

This evidence does not, perhaps, fully justify the high place given to Kaṇishka as a patron of Buddhism in the Mahāyana tradition. Yuan Chwang (Xuan Zhuang), in the seventh century, for example, describes a *stupa* and *sangharāma* (Buddhist monastery), built at Peshawar by Kaṇishka-rājā of Gandhāra. He then goes on to give a long account of the Great Council of 500 Buddhist sages convened by the same king in Kashmir to explain the Buddhist Canon, which they did in 'myriads of verses', essentially to lay down the Mahāyana interpretation. Two earlier Chinese pilgrims – Fahien (Fa Xian), *c.* 400, and Sung Yun, *c.* 518 – have far less to say about Kaṇishka, referring merely to the large tower (pagoda) he raised in Gandhara. Later Chinese accounts refer to Ka-ni-t'a, king of the Yue-ti (Yueh-chi), who gave hospitality to Ashvaghosha, the great Buddhist scholar, so that he could continue his work in peace in Kashmir. This king is supposed to be the same as Kaṇishka. All these legends must be treated with much caution despite the evidence of the 'Peshawar casket' found at the *stupa* in Peshawar that at least verifies part of the received accounts.

Yet, given the numerous deities and religious sects of his Bactrian and Indian subjects, the simultaneous display of attachment to Zoroastrianism, Shaivism and Buddhism was a prudent piece of policy for the Kushāns, especially if it could be combined with a cult of the divinity of the king and his line. One observes that in the Peshawar casket placed within a purely Buddhist *stupa*, Kaṇishka is represented as a deity standing between two Iranian gods, Miiro and Mao, the Sun and the Moon (*Figure 3.3*)! But the challenge of religious diversity was still perhaps easier to meet than that of geography.

It will be seen from our *Map 3.1* that Bactria stood on the very margins of the Kushān empire, and high mountains like the Hindukush and the Sulaiman range stood as barriers between the

FIGURE 3.3 Kaṇishka with two gods in attendance, in panel around the Peshawar casket. Archaeological Survey of India.

Kushāns' homeland and their Indian possessions. While, therefore, the Bactrian aristocracy might have formed the backbone of the Kushān ruling class (see *Chapter 3.5* below), the empire itself could hardly have been governed from a seat in Bactria. From *Map 3.1* it will also be seen that Kushān inscriptions (including those of Kaṇishka) are concentrated in two areas, viz. (1) in Gandhāra (between Peshawar and Taxila), and (2) at Mathura and in its vicinity. From the accounts of the three Chinese pilgrims about the Kaṇishka *vihāra*, it would seem as if

Poshapura or Pushpapura (modern Peshawar) was the main seat of Kaṇishka's government. There was also much building at Taxila under the Kushāns (the levels of remains mainly dated through finds of coins), and it is not clear why it has been held that 'it was not their capital' (A.H. Dani). Indeed it is quite possible that, as with the Mughal emperors, who for long treated Agra, Delhi and Lahore as their three major seats, Kaṇishka too had palaces and seats to move to and hold his court at, in different seasons, in order to ensure better control over various parts of the empire.

One evidence of the strength of Kaṇishka's administration is the way the era he instituted came to be used in inscriptions in Kharoshṭhī and Brāhmī, not merely in those set up by officials but also in the inscriptions of private individuals. As many as five Kharoshṭhī inscriptions bear his name, as well as the years 1, 11(2), 18 and 20 for dates. Numerous Brāhmī inscriptions, most of them from Mathura and its vicinity, are dated in years 2–5, 7–10, 12, 14–17, 19, 20 and 23. From these dates, it would seem that Kaṇishka's reign came to a close in or soon after year 23 or *c.* AD 183, according to the approximate date we have adopted for his accession (*c.* 160).

3.4. Huvishka

Kaṇishka's successor, represented in gold and copper coinage, is named Oeshki Koshano, a name which, in the form 'Oeshko', we also have in the Bactrian inscription at Airtam of the year 30. In Kharoshṭhī and Brāhmī inscriptions the name has the form Huvishka, with slight variants such as 'Hoveshka', 'Havashka' or 'Huvaksha', being obvious attempts to transcribe Oeshki. His inscriptions in the three scripts range from the year 25 to the year 60, the years actually recorded being 25, 26(2), 29, 30, 31(2), 33, 35(2), 38(2), 39(2), 40, 44, 45, 47, 48, 50, 51(2), 53, 58 and 60. Since the last year in Kaṇishka's inscriptions was 23, and the first dated one in Huvishka's successor Vāsudeva's reign belongs to year 64 or 67, Huvishka could be supposed to have reigned from *c.* AD 184 till a date between *c.* AD 220 and 224. He thus enjoyed a fairly long reign of nearly forty years.

We have, however, a puzzle which we must address before we try to present what we know about Huvishka from his inscriptions

MAP 3.1 The Kushān Empire

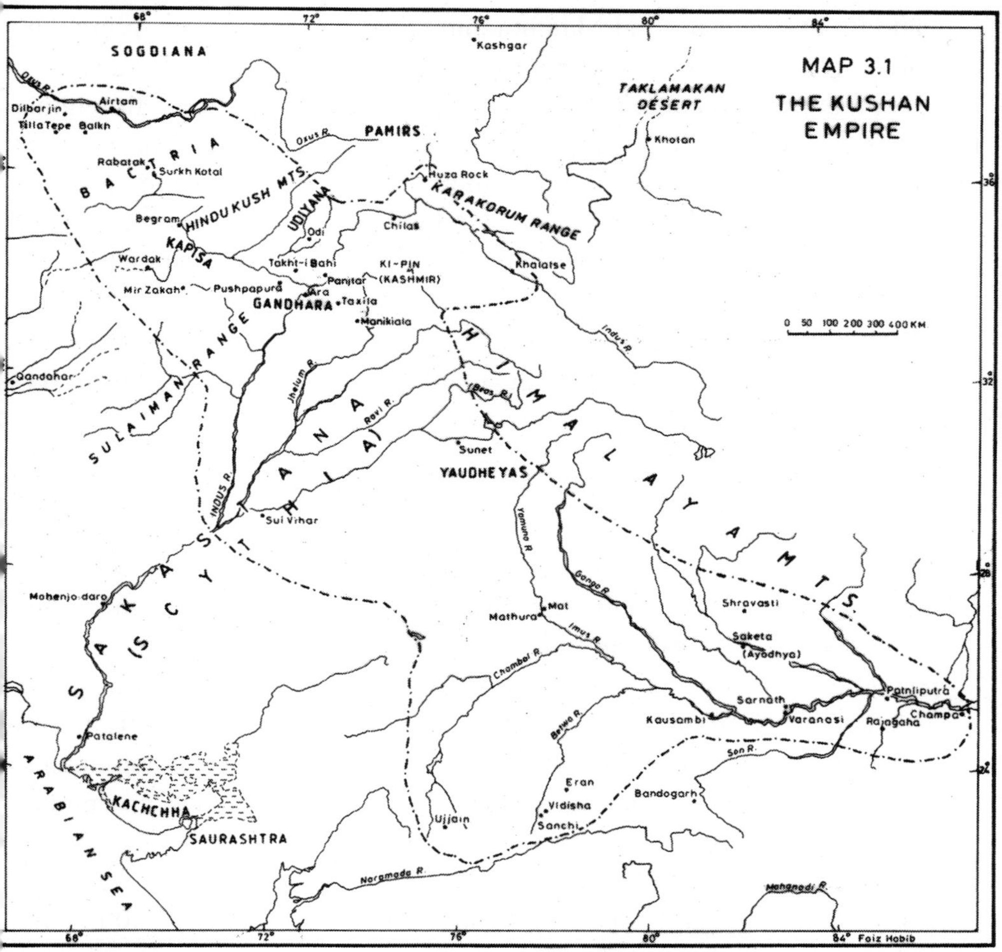

The line of dots and dashes shows the Kushān Empire at its greatest extent.

and coins. At Kamra, near Taxila, has been found a Kharoshṭhī inscription dated the year 20 or 30; one at Isapur near Mathura, of the year 24; and two of the year 28 at Mathura and Sanchi, respectively, giving the name of the Kushān sovereign as **Vāsishka** or Vajheshka. These years, if we ignore the reading of year 20 in the Kamra inscription, fall within the reign of Huvishka. They are geographically so spaced that it is not possible to hold that the Kushān empire was divided into the areas of authority of two contemporary sovereigns. Since the coins carry only the name 'Oeshki' and no inscription refers to two joint rulers, the only solution seems to be that the Vāsishka or Vajheshka is merely an alternative Prakrit transcription of Oeshki: if that name was pronounced in Bactrian as Hvashk, both Huvishka and Vāsishka would have been its passable representations in Prakrit.

This would also partly resolve the riddle posed by the Ara inscription, found near the fort of Attock on the Indus, dated the year 41 (in the middle of Huvishka's reign), giving the usual Kushān imperial titles to Kaṇishka, 'son of Vajheshka'. If Vajheshka is the same as Huvishka, it is not beyond the realm of possibility that here the scribe of a private well-inscription has by error put the names in reversed positions, when he ought to have written 'Vajheshka, son of Kaṇishka'. This is far more likely than that scribes in all the Vāsishka inscriptions and in the one at Ara have omitted to write the initial 100 in their dates. The assumption has been made to enable us to place them a century later and so avoid having to conceive of three contemporary joint-sovereigns; but proof that hundred years used to be omitted is wanting in the light of so many inscriptions that carry dates of above 100 in our period.

To return to Huvishka, his reign probably saw the Kushān empire at its apex of prosperity. This is illustrated, in the first place, by the abundance of his gold coinage. *Table 3.1* shows the numbers of gold coins of the Kushān emperors in three major museum collections.

Though it is true that Huvishka's gold coins seem hugely over-represented in the British Museum, his are nevertheless more in number than those of any other ruler in the other two collections as well; and in the aggregate, their number far exceeds the total of the gold coins of the other five rulers put together. Clearly, therefore, during his reign his treasury had abundant gold to mint and put into circulation.

Table 3.1 Kushān Gold Coins

	British Museum	*Indian Museum*	*Punjab Museum*	*Total*
Vima Kadphises	12.25	4.25	6.50	23.00
Kaṇishka	20.75	15.00	8.25	44.00
Huvishka	128.25	18.50	9.25	156.00
Vasudeva	22.50	13.25	4.75	40.50
Kaṇishka II	–	7.25	4.25	11.50
Vasudeva II	–	2.00	1.25	3.25
Total of museum collections	183.75	60.25	34.25	278.25

Note: Double staters and quarter-staters have been converted into staters arithmetically.

Source: Catalogues of Coins of the three Museums; see *Note 3.2*.

This, in turn, suggests his continuing control over the resources of an extensive domain.

The places where Huvishka's inscriptions are found also attest to the large areas he controlled. He is the only Kushān ruler with authority explicitly acknowledged in an inscription north of the Oxus – at Airtam in Uzbekistan. At Wardak in central Afghanistan, west of Kabul, he has left an inscription dated the year 51. Dani notes a 'Vajeshka' inscription at Chilas on the Indus before its great turn to the south beyond the western edge of the Western Himalayas. In the east there is an inscription of Huvishka at Shravasti; and to the south there is, as we have seen, a 'Vāsishka' inscription at Sanchi.

In his **religious policy** Huvishka seems to have taken care to follow in the footsteps of his predecessor. The 'god-house' ('bagolango', 'bagolaggo') at Surkh Kotal in Bactria, containing images of gods and Kushān emperors, was completed in year 31 under him. At Mat near Mathura, according to an inscription, Huvishka repaired the *devakula* ('god-house') built by his 'grandfather' Vima Kadphises, and possibly got his own image also installed there – this being the 'colossal' figure of a king which carries the inscription between its feet. Apart from patronizing the cult of divine status for the emperor,

Huvishka followed Kaṇishka in extending some patronage to Buddhism. An inscription at Mathura of year 51 (*c.* AD 221) refers to Huvishka and to 'the maharaja Devaputra *vihara*', apparently built by him. The same year, at Wardak, west of Kabul, an extreme western outpost of Buddhism was established with a *vihara* by an individual who did not forget to assign part of the merit to emperor 'Huveshka'. But again, like Kaṇishka, other religious affiliations were not forgotten. The Iranian deities Mao (Moon), Mioro (Sun) and Nana (goddess) are heavily represented on his coins, and he follows Kaṇishka also in so honouring Indian deities such as Okra (Shiva), Skanda and Vishākha. On fewer coins, the Greek gods Herakles and Hephaistos are also to be found. Curiously enough, the Buddha disappears now from the Kushān coinage.

3.5 Kushān Polity

The discovery and decipherment of Bactrian inscriptions of the Kushān emperors (down to Huvishka) in northern Afghanistan, crowned by the Rabatak inscription (*Extract 3.1*), has left no doubt about Bactria being the Kushān homeland, the base from which the dynasty made its conquests to form an empire. In this region inscriptions tell us of as many as five **'god-houses'** ('bagolango') where the images of the Kushān emperors were installed along with those of different deities – at Dasht-i Nawar, Dilbarjin, Rabatak, Surkh-Kotal and Airtam. These temples were large structures with special care taken to bring water to them through streams or canals. This heavy concentration of royal 'god-houses' in Bactria seems designed to make a special appeal to the local population or its higher classes, to repose loyalty in the ruling dynasty in view of its divine status. In their Indian possessions, the only such 'god-house' (*deva-kula*) known to have been constructed was at Mat, near Mathura, where too, apart from the gateway (*dārakoṭa*) and building or hall (*sabhā*) created to house the divine imperial images, provision was made of an adjacent garden (*ārāma*) and a tank (*pushkariṇi*) fed from a well (*udapānaṁ*). The Bactrian model duplicated here seems to suggest that it was established more to keep the Kushān bureaucracy at Mathura tied to their sovereign than to appeal to a wider circle, for which far more *devakulas* would have been needed. It is noteworthy that in the images here, the rulers maintain their Bactrian costume. In the famous Kaṇishka statue from this site at Mat, the king wears a gown, long shirt, trousers and boots, with no attempt made to Indianize his appearance (*Figure 3.2*). Perhaps the 'worshippers' at the royal shrine were also mostly fellow Bactrian courtiers and high officials, for whom this would precisely be the costume expected of a king. Yet there are Indianizations: the language used in the Mat *devakula* inscriptions is mixed Prakrit-Sanskrit and by the year 28, Brahmans are expected to appear at the *devakula*.

Our knowledge of those who served the Kushāns as their ministers, governors, commanders and civil **officials** is limited to what we learn about their offices and names from inscriptions. In Bactria the one officer we encounter is the *karalrang*, or governor. At Rabatak the official responsible for building the god-house was Shafar ('Shaphara'), the *karalrang*, aided by one Nukunzuk ('Nokonzoko') who led the rites of worship. At Surkh-kotal, where a fort and god-house were built under Kaṇishka, 'Nokonzoko' appears as the *karalrang* who completed the work. At Airtam, under Huvishka, the official who carried out the work was Shodila, the treasurer. All these officials were obviously Bactrians or, at least, Iranians, to judge by their names. So also was the scribe at Airtam, Miirozada.

As the Kushāns expanded out of Bactria, they doubtless encountered kingdoms, especially in remoter zones, whose submission they accepted and which thereafter continued to be ruled by their hereditary rulers. This is illustrated by the Odi inscription of Senavarman, who, as the local ruler of Swat valley, acknowledged Kajula Kadphises as his paramount sovereign. However, it is also true that such a situation is not indicated in the more populous areas of the Kushāns' Indian dominions from which most of their inscriptions have come to us. Here direct rule appears to have prevailed.

In their **Indian possessions** the Bactrian designation *karalrang* for the governor is not used. It is replaced by *mahākshatrapa/kshatrapa*, inherited from the Sakas. In two inscriptions on a Bodhisattva image at Sarnath, both dated year 3 of the Kaṇishka era, the first mentions Vanaspara and Kharapallana as *kshatrapas*, while the second styles Kharapallana as *mahākshatrapa* while continuing to designate the other as *kshatrapa*. It is possible to suppose from this that the pair were first jointly governing Varanasi (the town mentioned in the first inscription) as *k<u>sh</u>atrapas*, but soon afterwards one of them was made senior to the other. Both the personal names are Iranian. In the Manikiala inscription, near Taxila, of Kaṇi<u>sh</u>ka's 18th year, we have a reference the *kshatrapa* Veshpashi who was presumably the governor of Taxila. In another inscription from the same place, we are told of the *k<u>sh</u>atrapa* of Kavisha (Kapisha, or Kabul), left unnamed, but said to be the son of *k<u>sh</u>atrapa* Granavhasyaka. The names of the officials here too are Iranian.

The Manikiala inscription of Kaṇi<u>sh</u>ka's 18th year is also noteworthy in another respect: it describes one Lala as of the 'Gushaṇa' (Kushān) clan (*vasha*), but designates him as *daḍanāyaga* (Sanskrit *daṇḍanāyaka*, the staff-wielding chief) or military commander. We are told that he also served as the *horamurta* (Saka for 'treasurer') of the *k<u>sh</u>atrapa* Veshapashi, and so must have been subordinate to him. In the Shertala inscription (NWFP) of the year 39, one Bhāharaka is described as 'the Kushaṇa *shāhi's daḍanayaga*', while Pahaka was the *k<u>sh</u>atrapa.* One could suppose that these officials together governed Po<u>sh</u>apura or the Peshawar territory. In a later inscription from Mathura, of the year 74, in the reign of Huvi<u>sh</u>ka's successor Vāsudeva, we find a higher designation, *maha-dāṇḍanāyaka*, being used; the name of the holder of this title, Valāna, is again Iranian.

An apparently high office was that of *bakanapati* or *vakanapati*, charged at Mathura with the building of the 'god-house' at Mat under Vima Kadphises; that official bore the name of Huma<u>sh</u>pāla. In year 28 under Huvi<u>sh</u>ka the then *vakanapati*, Kharāsalerapati, son of Kanasarukamāna, is represented as making an endowment to feed Brahmans, the merit to accrue to his sovereign. The names of the officials are non-Indian and their Bactrian background is reflected in the use of the Macedonian month Gorpiaios.

There can be little doubt, therefore, that the higher ranks of the Kushān officials were dominated by Bactrians and other Iranic elements. While their inscriptions in India might be in Prakrit (increasingly influenced by Sanskrit), it is likely that 'Aria' or Bactrian remained for long a living language in their ranks. This is shown pre-eminently by their coinage, which, from Kaṇi<u>sh</u>ka onwards, dropped the Kharo<u>sh</u>ṭhī legends and shifted to solely Bactrian legends in Greek characters. This probably gave the Kushān empire its cohesiveness at the top, but was likely to weaken it immensely if Bactria and the regions adjacent to it, constituting the source of its ruling class and chief elements in the army, were lost. This happened soon after Huvishka's death, as we shall see presently.

We are not in a position to say anything about the composition and organization of the Kushān **armies.** Given the region from which their power expanded, the Kushāns' major advantage must have lain in their cavalry. We have seen above (*Chapter 1.3*) that the horse-bits must have given the Greek and Saka (Shaka) horsemen advantage over their Indian opponents. But cavalry everywhere still lacked the concave saddle, stirrup and horse-shoe. This can be confirmed from depictions of horsemen riding horses in friezes at Shahr-i Bahlol (NWFP), ascribed to Huvishka's time, as well as Mathura sculpture. But the Kushāns still have a place in the history of

FIGURE 3.4 Horseman using toe-stirrup. Mathura sculpture. V.A. Smith. See full panel in Figure 4.6.

FIGURE 3.5 Bodhisattva, Gandhāra sculpture, Taxila. J. Marshall.

stirrup, since a rope-loop hanging from the saddle-cloth, into which the horseman's toe (not simply the big toe) is tucked, is depicted on a Kushān-period sculpture at Mathura (*Figure 3.4*) and on a copper vase of the same time recovered from Kulu. A Kushān engraved gem shows what is believed to be a hook, rather than a looped rope, to serve as quasi-stirrup. Though neither of these had the efficacy of the iron stirrup of later times, the devices still evidence an effort made under the Kushāns to improve the efficiency of the horseman by providing some sort of foot-rest while riding.

The presence of numerous members of the ruling class coming from the Iranian world, which in Parthian times was itself greatly influenced by the culture of the Hellenistic and then Graeco-Roman world, helped to create new skills in art. The rise of **Gandhāra sculpture** in the north-west (the Taxila-Peshawar region) is confined mainly to Buddhist subjects, notably the Buddha and Bodhisattvas, but it nevertheless displays manifest influences of Graeco-Roman art of the first two centuries AD (see *Figure 3.5*). Such influence can also be seen in the remains of the imperial Kushān statuary of Mat and Mathura.

3.6 Vāsudeva and Later Kushāns

The last date on Huvishka's inscriptions being the year 60, while the earliest mentioning **Vāsudeva** as sovereign is dated 64 or 67, the latter must have succeeded Huvishka between *c.* AD 220 and 224 or 227. Vāsudeva is named in subsequent inscriptions dated years 74, 77, 80, 83, 84, 87, 93 and 98, so that his reign must have come to a close in or after *c.* AD 258. He could therefore have ruled like Huvishka for about forty years. His name is the only Indian name known to have been adopted in the Kushān family, it being also assigned to a successor of his. His coinage continued the style of his predecessors, using only Greek-Bactrian legends, in which his name appears as 'Bazodeo Koshano'. *Table 3.1* shows that the number of gold coins he issued was not much smaller than that of Kaṇishka, though far smaller than of Huvishka. His gold and copper coins have an extensive range: the copper coins are numerous around Mathura, and show heavy concentration at Taxila and at Mohenjo Daro in Sind. His coins also occur at find-spots extending further north-westwards up to Khwarizm on the lower course of the Oxus.

Vāsudeva's inscriptions, however, tell us a different story. They are all in Brāhmī script, and confined to Mathura and its environs. But even in the Ganga basin he might have lost much territory, for at Kausambi a local dynasty seems to have become independent by the year 81 (*c.* AD 241), with one of its rulers, Bhadramagha, leaving us an inscription of that date. But the crucial loss that the Kushān empire suffered was in the west.

According to the practically contemporary annals, the *San-kou-chih* of Che'n Shou (d. 297), the 'Great Yueh-chi' king Po-t'iao (Vāsudeva) sent an embassy in AD 230 to the Wei court in China. It is likely, from the continuing Chinese confusion of the Kushāns with the Great Yueh-chi owing to their earlier geographical proximity, that Vāsudeva was still master of Bactria. The embassy might have been sent for commercial reasons; but, as is more likely, it was really for the purpose of gaining support, or at least neutrality, from the Chinese court in the impending conflict with the Sassanids of Iran.

It is noteworthy that after Huvishka's Wardak vase inscription of year 51 (*c.* AD 211), no inscription in Bactrian or Kharoshṭhī has been discovered in the Panjab, NWFP or Afghanistan that mentions any Kushān ruler. In excavations at Begram, north of Kabul, Ghirshman established the end of Kushān occupation by much evidence of destruction at a particular level. In the preceding layer below, coins were found of Kaṇishka, Huvishka and Vāsudeva. The phase that followed the destruction was labelled 'Sassanian'. On the face of it, this suggests that the event of destruction occurred during the reign of Vāsudeva, whereafter the town was occupied by the Sassanians who were seeking to revive the glories of ancient Iran. In his inscription at Naqsh-i Rustam, the Sassanian king Shapur I says of his predecessor Ardashir I (226–41), that he subjugated territories in the east, including Merv and the Sakas; but the later historian Ṭabarī credits Ardashir with the conquest of Balkh as well, which would mean that he had also seized Bactria, the Kushān homeland. By referring to a later era whose epoch is placed at AD 232, some historians would place the conquest of Bactria and the establishment of the Sassanian branch of 'Kushān-shāhs' at about this date. More certain, however, is the claim made by Shapur I (241–71) in his Ka'ba-i Zardusht inscription (*c.* 260) of being the master of Kushanshahr (the Kushān region), its borders extending to Pushkapur (i.e. Poshapura, or Peshawar), Kash (Kashghar), Sughd (Sogdiana in Trans-oxiana) and Sash (Chāch or Tashkent). Considering the chronology of his reign, it is believed that the conquests occurred in the 240s.

Whether made in the 230s or 240s, these conquests fell within the reign of Vāsudeva, who had, as we have seen, come to the throne in or before AD 227. The Sassanids established a line of subordinate Kushān-shāhs whose coins in gold and copper are modelled in the first phase on those of Vāsudeva: they bear Bactrian legends, and contain on the reverse (as Vāsudeva's coins do) representations of Shiva and Nandi, the bull. One of the towns minting these coins is 'Bahlo' or Balkh, the historic capital seat of Bactria. Later, the Kushān-shāhs began minting coins of the Sassanid style with Pahlavi (Middle Persian) legends.

As we have suggested above (*Chapter 3.5*), the loss of Bactria and the rest of Afghanistan would have meant a critical blow to Kushān power, for now the Kushān kings in India were cut off from their cultural and ethnic homeland. Vāsudeva himself was transformed from an emperor of a large domain (as evidenced by the wide range of the find spots of his coinage) to the ruler of Mathura and its immediate vicinity. We lack evidence even for the continuance of his rule over Taxila in his later years.

Coins, found mostly in the Mathura region, show that Vāsudeva, whose last recorded year is 98 or *c.* AD 258, was followed by Kaṇishka II, Vāsudeva II and 'Baeshko' (which has been assumed by historians to represent Vāsishka, though the latter form is not actually found). These rulers too continued to use Bactrian legends on their coins and even issued gold coins, though with declining gold content. The exact order in which they should be placed is not clear. The only known inscription attributable to them is one possibly of the reign of Vāsudeva II, given the usual Kushān title of *devaputra shāhī*, and belonging to the year 170 (*c.* AD 330). However, since the author of the inscription is a Shaka, the year could be of the Shaka era and so correspond to AD 248, in which case the inscription could be referring to Vāsudeva I (see *Extract 3.2*).

Perhaps, the last reference to the Kushāns as an important contemporary dynasty occurs in Samudragupta's Allahabad pillar inscription, which cannot be dated earlier than AD 350. The first to be mentioned among those who sought conciliation with Samudragupta is the 'Devaputra-Shāhi-Shāhānushāhi', thus designating the Kushān ruler by his traditional titles. But the end was near. An inscription from Mathura of Chandragupta II, of Gupta year 61 or AD 380, shows that the last Kushān capital had by then been annexed to the Gupta empire.

3.7 Other Dynasties of the Third Century

The Kushān empire in north India and the Sātavāhana kingdom in the Deccan almost simultaneously underwent decline in the first half of the third century; and this provided opportunity to local or regional rulers to assert or enlarge their authority. Several appear to have done so by issuing coins, mainly in copper; and the existence of a few is also attested by inscriptions. It is to the latter that we shall mainly confine our attention.

Two such states seem to have arisen within territories included in the Kushān empire. A self-described Shaka chief Shrīdharavarman, who first used the Kushān designation of *mahādaṇḍanāyaka* and then the title of *mahākshatrapa*, has left two inscriptions dated in the Shaka era, corresponding to AD 279 and 293, in the **Vidisha** region (see *Chapter 1.3* above), so that by these years the region no longer recognized Kushān suzerainty. At **Kausambi,** near Allahabad, we have evidence of a line of rulers, beginning with Bhadramagha. These rulers use an era which is likely to be the Kushān era that had already been established in the area. Bhadramagha's earliest inscription is dated year 81 (*c.* AD 241), and so he must have become independent already during Vāsudeva's reign. His other inscriptions bear the years 86–88 and 90; and he is followed by Shīvamagha, Vaishravaṇa (year 107) and Bhīvavarmaṇa (years 130, 139). The dynasty lasted, therefore, till at least *c.* AD 299. Whether this line of rulers can be identified with the Magha dynasty of Kosala, described in the Purāṇas, is not certain, since there is no independent evidence that the Kausambi rulers held any part of Kosala.

To the south, at **Bandogarh** near the upper Son valley in Central India and at hilly sites around it, inscriptions have been found palaeographically similar to those of the Magha dynasty of Kausambi, which enable us to reconstruct a line of local rulers with some dates given in an unnamed era: Chitrasena, Vaishravaṇa, Bhīmaseṇa (years 51, 52), Jangata (year 80), Poṭhasiri (years 86–88) and Bhaṭṭadeva (year 90). Though it is possible that the dynasty used its own era, it is also possible that the Kushān era was employed, in which case the dates would run from *c.* AD 211 to 251. V.V. Mirahsi's theory that this dynasty is identical with the Magh dynasty of Kausambi does not seem to be tenable.

A state on the nature and history of which there has been much speculation is that of the **Yaudheyas.** In his Junagadh inscription of AD 150, Rudradāman claims to have 'destroyed the Yaudheyas' who had been filled with pride over their 'title of heroes among all Kshatriyas' (see our *Extract 1.3*). This is good evidence that by the middle of the second century, the Yaudheyas, as a kind of confederacy of Kshatriya chiefs, had obtained a certain amount of power in trans-Sutlej Panjab and Haryana where their copper coins are found. But their coinage itself belongs to a later time, probably the late third century, since it shows some influence of Kushān coinage. Two clay seals of the Yaudheyas, one from Sunet near Ludhiana, and the other from Jajjhar in Haryana, are palaeographically assigned to early fourth century. The Jajjhar seal, significantly, speaks of the 'Yaudheya *janapada*', the latter meaning a community or region. From this evidence only this much can be said, that the Yaudheya confederacy, remarkable in its not having a king, revived upon the decline of Kushān power; but this hardly justifies one's holding, as some historians (e.g. Altekar) do, that the Yaudheya 'republic' played a great role in overthrowing the Kushāns.

Alongside the revived state of the Yaudheyas there appear to have arisen chiefdoms in Rajasthan that are worth remembering, if for no other reason than that they began using in their inscriptions the Vikrama ('Krita') era of 57 BC. The earliest, dated 282 (= AD 226), is from Nandsa in southern Rajasthan, the ruler being Shrī Soma of the Mālava *gaṇa* (people). At Barnāla, eastern Rājasthan, an inscription is dated Krita 284 (= AD 228), but the ruler's name is damaged. At Badva (south-eastern Rajasthan), three pillar inscriptions, dated Krita 295 (AD 238), record the sacrificial rites organized by three sons of *mahāsenāpati* Bala. Perhaps *mahāsenāpati* here represents not a military commander but an independent chief.

In the Deccan, the decline of the Sātavāhanas created space

for the **Ikhāku** (Ikshvāku) dynasty whose main seat was at Vijayapuri or Nagarjunakonda, Andhra Pradesh, where most of the Ikhāku rulers' inscriptions are found. The inscriptions enable us to establish the genealogy and order of succession of the following rulers: (1) the founder Chāṁtamūla, from whose reign itself no inscriptions survive; (2) Vīrapurisadata, whose inscriptions range up to regnal year 24; (3) Ehuvala Chāṁtamūla, last inscription dated regnal year 24; and (4) Ruḍapurisadata, whose only dated inscription belongs to his regnal year 4. The calculation of a *vijaya* year in a 60-year cycle by which Vīrapurisadata is supposed to have been reigning in AD 273–74, and his successor Ehavala Chāṁtamūla in 333–34, is not now generally accepted; and the dynasty is placed in the third century AD largely on palaeographic grounds. The Ikhākus continued to use Prakrit in their inscriptions.

The sites of the Ikhāku inscriptions are confined to the region of the lower courses of the Krishna and the Godavari. Yet the dynasty claimed to have matrimonial alliances with the rulers of Ujjain and Vanavāsa (Banavasi, western Karnataka) and the *mahakshatrapas* (presumably Western Satraps). A curious inscription at Nagarjunakonda, of an Ābhīra ruler, Vasushena, in his 30th regnal year, refers to the past installation of god Ashṭabhujasvāmin with the aid of 'the Shaka Rudradāman of Avanti and Vishṇurudrashivalānanda Satakarṇi of Vanavāsa'. While it is not easy to interpret this inscription and explain the Ābhīra ruler's presence in Nagarjunakonda (had he supplanted the Ikhākus, or just paid them a visit?), the relationships of the Ikhākus with other rulers of fairly distant kingdoms appear to be confirmed by it.

The area of the Ikhāku kingdom ultimately passed into the possession of the Pallavas, whose capital was at Kanchipuram in Tamil Nadu. Their occupation of the area, however, seems to have taken place well after AD 300.

On **the western coast**, the Sātavāhana kingdom had a series of successor states. At Nasik, once its major seat, an inscription has been found of the Ābhīra ruler (*rajña*) Īshvarasena, dated his regnal year 9. How long the Ābhīra regime lasted in Nasik, we do not know. The tribe itself had an earlier presence in Gujarat, which in *Periplus*,

Section 41, is called 'Abiria' – and the *Periplus* was definitely composed before AD 106. But otherwise, the Ābhīras' history is clouded in obscurity.

Further south on the coast, Mahābhojas seem to have ruled at Kuda: our knowledge of them is confined to just two inscriptions of uncertain date.

Finally, at Banavāsi, the Chutu-Sātakaṇis established themselves. Vinhukaḍa Chutukulānand Satakaṇṇi has left two inscriptions, one of regnal year 1 at Malavalli and the other of year 12 at Banavāsi. We have seen that a ruler of the same line is mentioned in the Ābhīra prince's inscription at Nagarjunakonda. In the fourth century, the Chutu-Sātakaṇis were apparently supplanted by the Kadambas.

For south Indian political history down to AD 300, see *Chapter 2.4.*

TABLE 3.2 Chronology (all dates approximate)

	BC
Greek rule ends in Bactria, by	50
	AD
Tilla-tepe necropolis; cultural treasurers, Begram	25–50
Unification of Bactria under Kajula Kadphises	75
Pan Cha'o repels Kushān raid on Khotan, after Kushān annexation of Taxila and Kashmir	90
Vima Kadphises succeeds Kajula Kadphises	120
Kushān conquest of Sind completed; report of it submitted to Chinese court	127
Kaṇi<u>sh</u>ka succeeds Vima Kadphises; first year of Kushān era begins; Rabatak inscription	160
Last year recorded of Kaṇi<u>sh</u>ka's reign	183
First year recorded of Huvi<u>sh</u>ka's reign	185
Last Trans-Indus Kushān inscription: Wardak	211
Last year recorded of Huvi<u>sh</u>ka's reign	220

First year recorded of Vāsudeva's reign	224
Vāsudeva sends embassy to China	230
First Sassanid intrusion into Kushān empire: governorate of Kushānshāhs established	232
Kausambi lost by Kushāns: first dated inscription of Magha dynasty	241
Sassanid emperor Shapur I's conquest of western Kushān dominions completed by	250
Last recorded year of Vāsudeva's reign	258
Last dated Kushān inscription from Mathura	330
Mathura annexed to Gupta empire before	380

Extract 3.1
The Rabatak Inscription of Kaṇiṣhka
(Bactrian language, Greek script)

. . . [Means?] of the great salvation, Kaneshka Koshan, the righteous, the just, the all-powerful, the god worthy of worship, who has obtained worship from [the goddess] Nana and from all the gods, who has established the Year One [of a new era] as the gods pleased. And he replaced the Ionian [Greek] language [for edicts] with Aria [Iranian]. In Year One it [this edict] has been proclaimed unto 'Iunda' (India), unto the whole realm of the Shatris (Kshatriyas?), Koonadiano (?), Ozene [Ujjain], Zageda [Saketa], Kozambi [Kausambi], and Palabotra [Pataliputra], as far as Ziritambo [Shri-Champa]. Whatever rulers and potentates there are, he had them submit to his will, and all 'Iunda' [India] so submitted to his will. Then *shai* [= Persian *shāh*, king] Kaneshka commanded Shaphar [Shafar], *Karalrang* [city superintendent?] to erect the Nana god-house ('bagolango'), which is called . . . Water ('. . . *ab*') in the plain of Kayepa (?), for these deities ('*baga*'), of whom are Ziry Phara [Farrah?], the Lady Umma ('Omma'), in the lead, the lady Nana, Aoramozda [Ahuramuzda], Mazdooana, Sroshard, Narasa (and) Mihr – called Maaseno (Mahāsena?) and Bizago (Vishākha?). And he likewise gave orders to make images of these deities who are written (about) above, and then he ordered (them) to make (images) for these kings. For the *sha* (Persian *shāh*) Kozoula Kadphisa, his great grandfather, and for his grandfather Saddashkana, and for the *sha* Ooema Kadphisa, his father, and for himself, the *sha* Kaneshka. Then as the 'shaonanosha' (Persian *shahanshāh*, king of kings) and 'bogopoor' (son of god = *devaputra*) . . . had given orders to do, Shafar the *karalrang* made this god-house. [Then] . . . [X], the *karalrang,* Shafar, the *Karalrang* and Nokonzoko, led the worship as commanded. These deities, who are written about here – may they keep the 'shaonanosha' (king of kings), Kaneshka Koshan, for ever healthy, safe and victorious, and [ensure for] the son of god authority over the whole of 'Iunda' (India) from the year one to the year thousand thousand. He founded the god-house in the Year One till when the great 'Aria' year [era] had been in use. . . [further text illegible]

Note: The translation above has been framed by comparing N. Sims-Williams's decipherment and rendering with those of B.N. Mukerjee (for details of which publications, see *Note 3.2*). While Mukherjee's decipherment and translation extends beyond Sims-Williams's, a major difference is that instead of the name of Saddashkana as Kaṇishka's grandfather, Sims-Williams reads 'Ooema Taktoo shao' – i.e. Vima Taktu the *sha* – without indicating any doubt about the reading. We have followed Mukherjee here and at some other places as well, but not in the last portion that Sims-Williams held to be illegible. The use of the word *sha* for Kaṇishka and his predecessors in this inscription disposes of the theory that the Kushān inscriptions in which the term *shāhi* occurs must belong to the time of Vāsudeva or later.

Extract 3.2
A Problematical Mathura Sandstone Inscription (mixed Sanskrit and Prakrit)

On the third day of the second 2 fortnight of the winter of the regnal year 100+70, [in the reign] of *rājatirāja devaputra Shāhī* Vāsudeva, on this date, the image of *Chakra* is installed (by) Tajahmara, the son of Saka Mahadita.

Note: This inscription from a San Francisco museum, noticed by B.N. Mukherjee, is given here to indicate the kind of puzzles some inscriptions pose. Does it refer to Kaṇishka year 170, indicating thereby that it belongs to the reign of Vāsudeva II, a Kushān ruler known otherwise only from coins; or is it dated in the Shaka era, since the author of the inscription is a Shaka? In the latter case, it should belong to AD 248, which, given our date for the inception of the Kaṇishka era (*c.* AD 160), would correspond to year 88 of that era and so belong to the reign of Vāsudeva I.

Note 3.1
Kushān Chronology

One major problem of post-Mauryan history is that of the dates of the Kushān dynasty. From Kaṇishka onwards, there are numerous inscriptions containing the names of Kushān emperors that are dated in years running almost continuously from year 1 to 98. The Rabatak inscription (*Extract 3.1*) has fully established what had so far been assumed only as a probability, that the beginning of the era marked Kaṇishka's accession. The major difficulty is to convert the years of this era into those of the Christian era that would place the Kushāns in the general chronological framework. Suggestions hitherto made about the date of the epoch (or beginning) of Kaṇishka's era in terms of years of the Christian era have been most varied. A large body of scholars, including the major historian of the Kushāns, B.N. Mukherjee, have held the view that Kaṇishka succeeded to the throne in AD 78, and that the Shaka and Kaṇishka eras are therefore the same. Others have proposed later dates: *c.* AD 100 (Joe Cribb); AD 127 (H. Falk); AD 128 (Sten Konow); AD 134 (Janos Harmatta); AD 144 (R. Ghirshman) and even AD 278 (R.G. Bhandarkar, who initiated the now recurring hypothesis of 'missing hundreds' in the dates of certain inscriptions).

It is not possible here to give all the arguments for and against each thesis. But the problem itself cannot be ignored since we have, after all, to decide for ourselves where in the order of historical sequence the Kushāns are to be placed. We have ourselves found the best niche for the epoch of the Kaṇishka era to be around AD 160, and, in this note, reasons for this are set out as briefly as possible.

The Rabatak inscription (*Extract 3.1*) has clarified what had hitherto been inferred from the numismatic evidence, that Kajula Kadphises and Vima Kadphises preceded Kaṇishka as Kushān emperors. It follows that the Kushān emperor (not further named) to whose time belong the Panjtar inscription of year 122 and the Taxila silver-scroll inscription of year 136, the latter specifically assigned to the Azes era, was Kajula Kadphises. Vima Kadphises is excluded, since his inscription at Khalatse (Ladakh) is dated as late as the year 187 or 184. Now the beginning of the reign of Azes, as Percy Gardner pointed out long ago, cannot, for orthographic reasons (shapes of Greek letters on coins of Azes I), be dated previous to 30 BC and not much later than AD 8 (see *Chapter 1.2*). Given this time-bracket, year 184 of the Azes era cannot be placed earlier than AD 154. If, therefore, Vima Kadphises was still ruling in AD 154, the beginning of the Kaṇishka era cannot possibly be placed before that date. This accords with the implications of a report in the Chinese annals that the Great Yueh-chi (Kushān) king Po'tiao sent an embassy to China in AD 230 (see *Chapter 3.6*). The description fits only Kushān emperor Vāsudeva ('Bazodeo'), whose inscriptions bear dates from years 64 to 98 of the Kaṇishka era. Even if he sent the embassy in his last known year, the epoch of the Kaṇishka era could not be earlier than AD 132. The same synchronism sets the lower possible date as well: Vāsudeva's predecessor Huvishka's last date is year 60, so that even if Vāsudeva succeeded him in that year and immediately thereafter sent his embassy to China, the beginning of the Kaṇishka era cannot be placed later than AD 170. The last Kushān inscriptions in Bactria are dated years 30 and 31, and the inscription at Wardak in central Afghanistan, year 51. This makes it certain that the area remained under Kushān control until year 51 of the Kaṇishka era. Now, even if we assume that the Sassanian conquest of this area, claimed in Shāpur I's Ka'ba-i Zardusht inscription of *c.* AD 260, took place no earlier than AD 250, one must allow at least 51 years of earlier Kushān rule from the date of Kaṇishka's accession onwards, so that his accession cannot by any means be dated after AD 199. In fact, it is possible that the Sassanian conquest of Afghanistan took place as early as AD 232, and that would place the lower limit for the beginning of the Kaṇishka era at AD 181.

Given these indications, the narrowest range within which the epoch of the Kaṇishka era can be placed is AD 154–70. Further precision does not seem possible. Our placing of it at *c.* AD 160 is simply due to the belief that the Kushān conquests in central India, including that of Ujjain, that Kaṇishka proclaims in his Rabatak inscription of his year 1, are unlikely to have taken place before Rudradāman's inscription of AD 150 (actually, some time after AD 150) (see *Extract 1.3*), where the same region is held to be under his suzerainty – and we need to allow some years to pass before the Kushān conquest occurred.

So far as one can see, this date is not in conflict with the other circumstances that are usually discussed while considering Kushān chronology, such as the influence of Roman coinage on Kushān mintage, the impact of Graeco-Roman sculpture on Kushān-period art, Roman and Kushān coins in common hoards, palaeographic changes, etc. Indeed, the Brāhmī characters of Kushān inscriptions are so close in shapes to the Gupta-period Brāhmī, that late second century dates for Kaṇishka's inscriptions at Mathura suit such affinities much better than any earlier dates.

Note 3.2

Bibliographical Note

The single major work on the Kushān empire is B.N. Mukherjee, *The Rise and Fall of the Kushāna Empire*, Calcutta, 1988, a product of vast learning. In Janos Harmatta (ed.), *History of Civilization of Central Asia*, Vol. II, UNESCO, Paris, 1994, chapters 11, 12, 14, 15 and 17 by various authors deal with different aspects of Kushān history and culture.

The Kharoshṭhī and Brāhmī inscriptions, with texts and translations and minimum commentary, are collected together in Satya Shrava, *The Dated Kushāna Inscriptions*, New Delhi, 1993. The standard collection of Kharoshṭhī inscriptions of the period is Sten Konow (ed.), *Corpus Insriptionum Indicarum*, II: *Kharoshṭhī Inscriptions*, Calcutta, 1929, reprint, New Delhi, 1991. For the Odi inscription of Senavarman, a relatively recent discovery, see *Journal of Asiatic Society (of Bengal)*, XXIII (12), 1981, pp. 152–59. The Kushān inscriptions in Bactrian have been conveniently brought together (texts and translations) by J. Harmatta in the *History of Civilizations of Central Asia*, Vol. II (above cited), pp. 422–33; on pp. 417–21, he also attempts to decipher and translate the text in an unknown language and script, that is part of a trilingual inscription at Dasht-i Nawar. The important Rabatak inscription in Bactrian discovered in 1993 was published in *Silk Road Art and Archaeology* (not unfortunately available at many Indian libraries), Vol. 4 (1996), pp. 75–142, with translation and commentary by Nicolas Sims-Williams and Joe Cribb, whereafter B.N. Mukherjee devoted a whole monograph to it (*The Great Kushāna Testament*, Indian Museum, Calcutta, 1995/1997).

Our *Table 3.1* is based on three catalogues containing lists of Kushān coins, viz.: Percy Gardner, *The Coins of the Greek and Scythian Kings of Bactria and India in the British Museum*, London, 1886, Indian reprint, New Delhi, 1971; V.A. Smith, *Coins of Ancient India: Catalogue of the Coins in the Indian Museum, Calcutta*, Vol. I, Oxford, 1906, Indian reprint, Delhi, 1972; and R.B. Whitehead, *Catalogue of Coins in the Panjab Museum*, Vol. I, *Indo-Greek Coins*, Oxford, 1914, photo-reprint, Chicago, 1969.

On Tilla Tepe (Bactria) in pre-Kushān (or early Kushān) times, Victor Sarianidi, *Bactrian Gold: From the Excavations of Tillya Tepe Necropolis in Northern Afghanistan*, Leningraad, 1985, is a detailed and comprehensive report on a splendid find.

In post-Sātavāhana Deccan, an important position was occupied by the Ikhākus (Ikshvākus). In *Nagarjunakonda,* Vol. II (*The Historical Period*), ed. K.V. Soundara Rajan, ASI, New Delhi, 2006, a historical sketch of the Ikhāku dynasty is provided by R. Subrahmanyam (pp. 8–88); and the inscriptions of the dynasty, as published in *Epigraphia Indica*, are collected together, pp. 539–89. It has to be noted that the report was prepared in 1992, and that it omits Ikhāku inscriptions found at sites other than Nagarjunakonda.

Irfan Habib and Faiz Habib, *Atlas of Ancient Indian History*, New Delhi, 2012, contains a detailed political map (Map 8), which, along with the chapter for the map (Chapter 8), may be consulted for the Kushān empire and contemporary dynasties.

4

Economy, 200 BC – AD 300

4.1 Forest and Horticulture

There is some evidence for the great extent of land still occupied by **forests**, which also implies that only a correspondingly restricted area had been brought under the plough as yet. The *Arthashāstra* of Kauṭilya, which probably received its final shape no earlier than mid-second century AD (see *Mauryan India* in this series, Note 1.2), tells us (2.2.15–16) that elephants of an inferior kind were to be found in Surāshṭra (modern Saurashtra) and Pañchanada (Panjab). These two regions must then have contained forests large enough for wild elephants to have roamed in them. No subsequent account ever mentions elephants being found in these regions. Another indication of the large sway of the forest is the attention the *Arthashāstra*, 2.11.78–96, devotes to animal skins obtained from various forest animals, placing them as items of apparel above all categories of textiles, for which latter see *Extract 4.4*. Hunters of wild animals and workers in skin or leather must, therefore, have been quite numerous; they formed a substantial portion of the outcaste *jātis* specified by occupation in the *Manusmriti* (X.32.30) – a work that cannot be earlier than the second century AD (see note to *Extract 1.4*).

It must be borne in mind that, as settled agricultural population expanded, so correspondingly, through the surplus extracted from agriculture a large market was created for **forest produce**. This included elephants caught for domestication and skins of forest animals. The *Arthashāstra*, 2.11.43–55, mentions various forest localities from which sandal-wood was obtained. The names of most of these regions are unheard of, but western Karnataka and Assam appear to be included. Aloes-wood from Assam ('Kāmarūpa') and Sri Lanka

('Pārasamudra') is described as another forest product apparently commanding a large market.

Alongside greater exploitation of forest produce came expanding domestication of forest trees, and so **horticulture**. Ashoka's inscriptions (Pillar Edict VII and Queen's Edict) contain the earliest epigraphic references to mango-groves (see *Mauryan India*, in this series, p. 116). In post-Mauryan India, the most remarkable development in horticulture appears to be the arrival of the *coconut* tree from South-east Asia. The earliest archaeological evidence of coconut fibre (coir) in India has come from the port of Arikamedu (Tamil Nadu), the find dated to late first century BC. In two Nasik inscriptions (*c.* AD 100), the *kshatrapa* Nahapāna is acclaimed as the generous donor of 32,000 stems of coconut trees (*nālīgera*), while his son-in-law Ushavadāta donated 8,000 coconut-tree stems to members of various religious sects. As D.D. Kosambi points out, coconuts on the western coast were still a novelty, since the *Periplus* of the Erythraean Sea (pre-AD 106), despite being such a detailed navigational and commercial memoir of the Arabian Sea ports, fails to notice the plant and its fibre that came to be so much used in shipping a few centuries later (see also below, *Chapter 4.10*).

The *Periplus*, Sections 56 and 63, reports *betel-nut* as grown in western Karnataka and Kerala, and in Bengal. There was much trade in this necessary ingredient of *pān* (betel-leaf), an addiction to which was already spreading among the wealthier strata of the population.

Groves and plantations represent a different kind of property than fields producing annual crops, for they required, unlike the latter, a long period of initial investment since trees take many years before they produce fruit. The presence of orchards could thus usually indicate the presence of a higher rural class distinct from ordinary peasants (see below, *Chapter 4.3*).

4.2 Agriculture

Plough-based agriculture seems now to have been firmly established. *Figure 4.1* reproduces the sculptured Kushān-period representation of an ox-drawn **plough**, which, after four millennia of use, is only now in full retreat before tractors. The *Manusmriti* (X.84), while

FIGURE 4.1 **Peasant with plough, Gandhāra sculpture.** D.D. Kosambi.

condemning the handling of the plough, describes it as a 'wooden (implement) with iron point that injures the earth and its creatures'. There is no proof that the draw-bar and the circular movement of cattle for purposes of threshing or oil-milling had been introduced as yet; the early hand-mills at Taxila are still semi-rotary, so that even for flour-milling the fully rotary querns were still some time away.

The *Arthashāstra*, II.24.12–14, mentions a number of **crops** according to times of sowing, and Table 3.1 in *Mauryan India* (p. 115) in this series reproduces a list of as many as nineteen crops based on its testimony (including sugarcane and long pepper mentioned in it elsewhere). This list stands for our period as well, given the date that is now ascribed to the completion of the *Arthashāstra*.

One important change for which evidence comes only from the first century BC was the introduction of transplantation in the cultivation of rice, noticed by Migellus, who is quoted by Strabo (XV.1.18). Cotton is excluded from the *Arthashāstra's* list of crops because it was apparently not still annually sown, the fibre being harvested from perennial plants. It is possible that in our period, the cultivation of the crop on an annual basis might have begun. In the passage on textile products from the *Arthashāstra*, 2.11.97–118, reproduced in our *Extract 4.3*, there appears to be a distinction implied between cotton out of which muslin yarn was made and its ordinary variety or varieties. The distinction occurs frequently in the *Periplus* of the Erythraean Sea, Sections 41, 48, 49 and 51. It is thus clear that continuous cultivation of cotton had by now led to many specialized varieties of the plant, and it is not unlikely, therefore, that it was also being converted into an annual crop.

It is likely that from sugarcane, liquor began to be produced through the so-called Gandhāra stills found at Shaikhan Dheri (Charsadda, NWFP) and Taxila, dated to the beginning of the Christian era. This is the earliest evidence of **distillation** in India, though the stills of the Gandhāra type (*Figure 4.2*) could only have produced weak alcohol.

The *Periplus*, Section 39, reports indigo being exported from Barbaricum from the Indus mouths; and this may be taken as evidence for indigo cultivation in central Sind (Sehwan region), a prominent indigo-producing area in Mughal times. The *Periplus*, Section 56, tells us that pepper was exported in great quantities from Muziris (Kerala), and this implies that there was already extensive cultivation of round pepper (to be distinguished from long pepper) on the Malabar coast. This was to become, in later centuries, a great article of world trade.

As the number of cultivated crops multiplied, various crops needed considerable watering, such as wheat, sugarcane and cotton, besides rice, particularly in areas under lighter rainfall and away from floodland. Besides wells, other **irrigation** works began to be constructed. Rudradāman's Junagadh inscription of AD 150 (our *Extract*

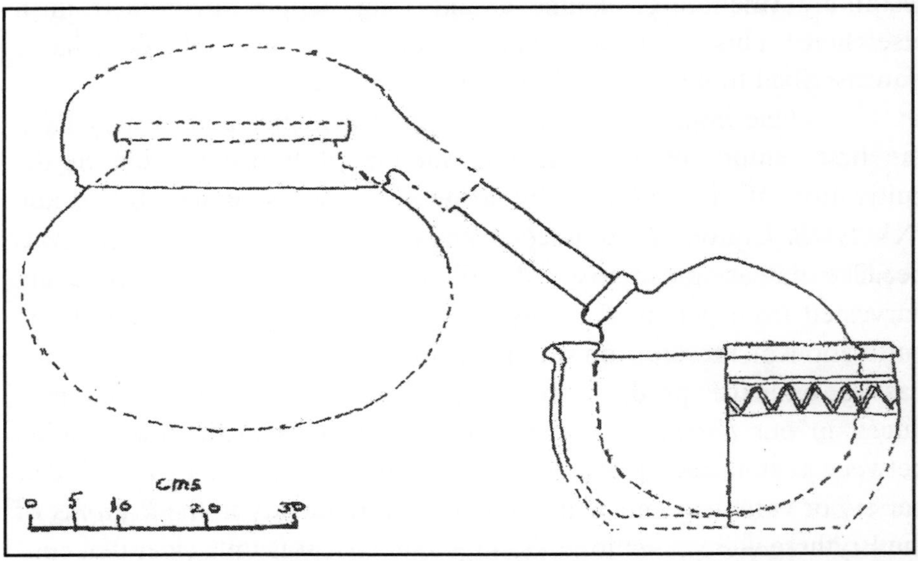

FIGURE 4.2 Gandhāra still. Reconstruction based on finds at Shaikhan Dheri, NWFP. F.R. Allchin. The liquid in the alembic on the right was heated, and the vapours were then led by the pipe to the head of the receiver into which the liquor-drops fell as the vapours cooled.

1.3) tells us how the destruction of the Mauryan-built dam of Girnar left 'the people (*prajā*) . . . loudly lamenting', obviously because of the loss of water that came to their fields through its conduits. It was now rebuilt. On the other side of the peninsula, in Orissa, Khāravela in his Hathigumpha inscription of the first century BC, speaks of a canal (*paṇāḍi*) which the Nanda ruler had laid out and now Khāravela restored (*Extract 2.2*). In the south a reservoir constructed in a village in Bellary district by a *gahapati* ('head of household') is described in the Myakadoni inscription of second century AD (*Extract 4.3*). Incidentally, the two-tank system for desilting at Sringaverapura on the Ganga in Uttar Pradesh, though quite ingenious, was designed for the provision of drinking water and had no irrigational purpose.

One can imagine that wells were still the main source of irrigation, despite the evidence we have for a dam and a canal. To draw up water from wells, pulleys (with water either drawn by hand, or by oxen that were made to move away and back along short walk-ways) had apparently been in use since Vedic times. An early version of the *Pañchatantra* (*c.* AD 300) probably gives us the first reference to the *araghaṭṭa* or a wheel carrying pots (*ghaṭṭa*) tied to the ends of its spokes (*ara*), a device known in technical language as 'noria'. This could be used to draw water from a tank or a well, with the spokes pushed by the hands of the operators. Its further development into *sāqiya* or the Persian wheel, with a pot-garland and, then, a gearing mechanism, was to take almost a further one thousand years (see *Technology in Medieval India* in this series, pp. 8–14). Obviously, hard human labour was still required for certain methods of water-lift in use in the early centuries of the Christian era.

4.3 The Agrarian Order

As the cultivation of profitable agricultural crops, needing much greater preparation of land and irrigation, expanded, the possession of cattle, needed for both ploughing and drawing water from wells, began to distinguish the **upper-class villagers** from the **ordinary mass.** There were to be found, on the one side, the 'plough owners' or the 'men-living-in-houses', whom we shall soon meet, and the ordinary body of villagers and other indigent sections of the population. In some areas that were favourably situated, agricultural land might have begun to carry a price. About AD 100, the Shaka prince U<u>sh</u>avadāta, in one of his Nasik cave inscriptions, claims to have purchased 'a field' (*k<u>sh</u>etra*) for the price (*mula*) of 4,000 *kāhāpaṇas* (small silver coins) from a Brahman named Ashvabhuti. Soon afterwards, a Sātavāhana inscription refers to a field (*kheta*) in a named village (*gāma*) that had been owned by the same U<u>sh</u>avadāta (now dispossessed, see *Chapter 1.3*). In another inscription, a private individual donates a field (*kheta*) in a particular village to provide the clothing for an ascetic living in a Nasik cave. In these cases, we may well be encountering true land-owners who could sell or give away agricultural land.

The *Milindapañho* (*Extract 4.1*) paints for us a picture of the village divided into two classes. On one side were the *kuṭipurise*, 'men of houses', distinct apparently from those who lived in huts. The latter comprised ordinary peasants (*gāmika*) and other classes of still lower sort – slaves, both women (*dāsī*) and men (*dāsa*), hired labourers (*bhataka*) and servants (*kammakarā*). Unlike the *kuṭipurise*, and, put on the same plane as 'oxen, buffalo, sheep, goats and dogs', they did not at all count in the affairs of the village.

This division into the dominant and the repressed groups within villages could have had roots both in the caste system and the structure of state power. But it was also sustained by the increasing importance of cattle for agriculture with the spread of the use of the plough, and so of those who owned them. In the third century, the Ikhāku ruler Vasithiputa Siri Chaṁtamūla is eulogized in many inscriptions as the giver away not only of much gold, but also of 'a hundred thousand cattle (*go*) and a hundred thousand ploughs (*hala*)'. In the *Kāmasūtra*, the villagers who could exploit the women of the poorer strata include 'plough-owners' (*halotthav<u>ri</u>thi*) – persons who owned, but apparently got others to labour at, their ploughs. An inscription from Selavardi, Maharashtra, may here be considered. This records the gift of a cave jointly by the wife of a *hālakiya* and *kuḍubika* (plough-owner and householder) and their son, who is described as a *gahapati* (head of house). As D.D. Kosambi points out, the 'plough-owner' must have belonged to the gentry, not the labouring class; in fact, all the three terms used here were clear designations for men of the upper land-owning rural class.

The passage from the *Kāmasūtra* (second–third century AD),

which we present in our *Extract 4.2*, shows strikingly how the upper groups within the village could treat those situated beneath them. Women from the poorer classes could be subjected to sexual advances when they came to work for the village headman (*grāmadhipati*), the local official (*āyukta*) or the plough-owner. Such women came to render forced labour (*vi<u>sh</u>ṭikarma*) for these men; they also had to carry material in or out from the men's store-houses; repair or clean their houses; and work on their fields (*k<u>sh</u>etra-karma*). They took cotton, wool, flax, hemp and tree-bark from these men's houses to spin into yarn, which they had to bring back. The women were also vulnerable when they came to them to buy or sell: apparently, the men also controlled such commerce as existed in the village. No record exists of how the ordinary labourers, the slaves and servants of whom the *Milindapañho* speaks, were treated. The *Kāmasūtra* lifts the curtain on only a part of rural misery; but it, perhaps, allows us to imagine the rest. In the *Manusm<u>r</u>iti*, X.83–84, manual agricultural work is decreed to be blameworthy; and the process whereby the population actually working in the fields was pushed into a Shūdra status was now, perhaps, quite well-advanced, if not complete.

Apart from the village oligarchs' exploitation of the lower strata of the village population, there was the pressure of **revenue** and other demands from the state and its agents. We may recollect that Khāravela, in his Hathigumpha inscription of the late first century BC, speaks of *kara* (tax) and *vaṇa* (cesses) as the two major exactions levied by the state (*Extract 2.2*). Rudradāman, in his Junagadh inscription of AD 150, refers to *bali* (tax), *shulka* (tolls) and *bhāga* (share of crop) as the three sources of filling the treasury, and to *kara*, *vi<u>sh</u>ṭi* (forced labour) and *praṇayakriya* (benevolences) as additional levies that could be imposed on people of town-and-country (*paurajānapada*) (*Extract 1.3*). Ashoka's Rummeindi pillar inscription shows that *bali* and *bhāga* were both imposed on the village of Luṁmini. Ashoka had remitted *bali* and reduced the *bhāga* to one-eighth (*aṭha-bhāga),* this being presumably the share of the crops harvested. What size the *bhāga* or the land-tax under any other name could take in cases where it was not especially reduced, is indicated by the statement in the *Arthashāstra* (V.2.2) that a king could demand in tax a third or fourth of the produce. While the *Arthashāstra*'s statement applies to both Mauryan times and our period, the *Manusmriti*, X.118, a text more definitely datable to second century AD, allows a Kshatriya chief or ruler, when in distress, to take a fourth part of the produce, as if this was the maximum limit of permissible taxation. In actual fact, however, the tax might have varied according to the armed capacity of the rulers and the efficiency of their administration. This would all the more have been the case if the state assigned different parts of its possessions to individual officials and left it to them to collect whatever they could to maintain themselves and their retainers, while presumably delivering a contracted amount to the royal treasury.

Such an arrangement is implied by an inscription of the 8th year of reign of the Sātavāhana ruler, Siri-Pulumāvi, found at Myakadoni, Bellary district, Karnataka (*Extract 4.3*). Here, the *ahāra* (district) of Sātavāhani is described as the *janapada* of *mahāsenāpati* Khaṁdanāka, and the particular village (*gāma*) within it, where a 'head-of-house' (*gahapati*) had built a reservoir, is said to belong to a *gumika* (military officer?) Kumāradata. The inference can be drawn that the *mahāsenāpati* or commander held the province in service tenure (i.e. to provide him with his own income and resources for maintaining his troops), and that the village had been sub-assigned by him to a captain of his. D.D. Kosambi has treated this record as the first piece of evidence for what he calls 'Feudalism from Above'.

The *gahapati* who set up the inscription should not, however, himself be overlooked. Obviously, the same as *kuṭipurise* of the *Milindapañho*, he had resources enough to build a reservoir in his village. The state's connection with rural gentry of this sort was crucial for the collection of whatever tax, whether amounting to one-fourth of the crop or more, that its officials sought to collect from the villages. It may be imagined that in the tax so collected, the *gahapatis*, as the influential villagers, duly claimed their share, or simply enjoyed tax immunities. We may recall here the statement in Khāravela's Hathigumpha inscription with regard to that ruler's remission of taxes levied on the various castes (*jātis*) of the *porajānapada* (Sanskrit: *paura-jānapada*). In turn, they could compel the ordinary villagers to meet the full tax demand imposed on them.

There were outsiders, too, who entered the village to secure tax payment. Promises made to recipients of grants of village lands in

Sātavāhana inscriptions of *c.* AD 100 in the Nasik and Karle caves imply that in ordinary villages royal officers entered freely and seized ('touched') villagers' possessions, or had saline soils dug up for salt, while other higher officers (*raṭha*) also descended on the village to do whatever they wished.

The **grants** of fields and villages which are mentioned in the inscriptions of Kshatrapa Nahapāna's son-in-law, Ushavadāta, and of the Sātavāhanas (second century AD) are mainly conferred on Brāhmaṇas, the Buddhist monastic establishments and other ascetics. These grantees, apparently made immune from paying taxes, are not restrained in any manner in the way they chose to conduct themselves with respect to the cultivators of the grant-lands. Probably, they were expected to extort whatever they could from them, except in cases where, as is mentioned in one inscription, the land was as yet uncultivated. Of that they were, in any case, full masters. In our period, the class of such grantees was probably not large. No inscription of the Kushān emperors, for instance, records any such grant, despite the fact that they held the larger part of northern India for over a century. Thereafter, however, such land-grants became customary in almost every part of India.

4.4 Craft Tools and Techniques

Before presenting our information on extractive and artisanal industries, it may be useful to consider separately changes in craft technology that came about in our period, and could have affected efficiency in both mining and manufacture.

In the excavations at Sirkap, Taxila, datable to first century AD, were found three iron **tools** that must surely have added considerably to the efficiency of craftsmen in different branches of work, viz. tongs, pliers and scissors – all based on the same mechanical principle of two arms crossing each other at a central point, but put to different uses (*Figure 4.3*). They had come into use during first century BC/AD in the Graeco-Roman world, and until other discoveries are made, India would seem to have received them from that source. Among Indian texts, the word *kartari* for scissors occurs in Charaka, who, by a late Chinese tradition, was a contemporary of Kaṇishka, and so could not have lived before the second century AD. All these were simple devices designed to concentrate power for grappling and cutting

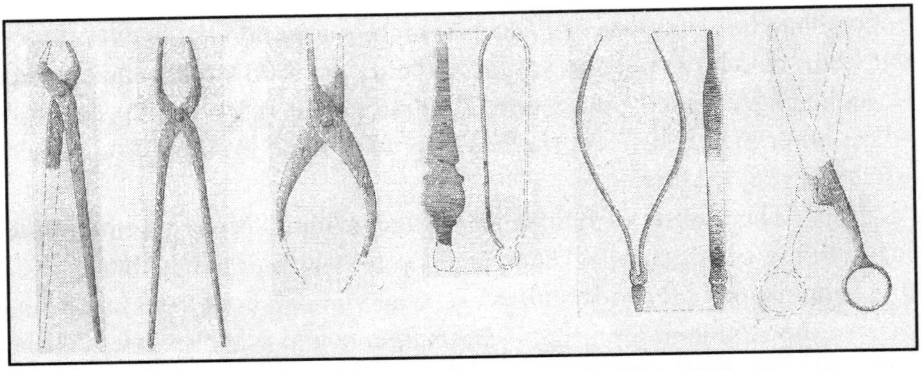

FIGURE 4.3 Pliers, tongs and scissors, Sirkap, Taxila. J. Marshall.

purposes. Scissors also implied the presence of shears, which are convenient cutting tools for trimming trees and plants. At Tilla Tepe (north Afghanistan, first century AD) a gold buckle has been found, and buckles are also shown on shoe-straps on Kaṇishka's Mat statue (second century), so that this useful fastening device too had now been introduced.

Another invention, that of the *scutch-bow*, proved to be of considerable consequence for the textile industry. Before being spun, cotton has to have its fibres separated, in order to be rendered suitable for spinning. This can be achieved crudely by beating bits of it with a stick. It was discovered in India some time in the early centuries of the Christian era that the same result could be achieved much better by subjecting puffs of raw cotton to the vibrations of bow-strings. So came into use the carding or scutch-bow. A reference in the *Mahājanaka Jātaka* to *kappāsa-pothanadhanuka*, or 'cotton-striking bow', is decisive, whereas an allusion in the *Milindapañho* to carding (*piñjitaṁ*) is less definite, though the word used here for carding *was* later on used for bow-scutched fibre. Such a seemingly simple device could have improved the quality of spun yarn and thereby created room for a widening variety of textiles.

In **metallurgy** archaeological finds have indicated two important developments, which might, indeed, have had an earlier history (and so have already been mentioned in *Mauryan India* in our series), but are probably to be assigned to the beginning of our period. The first is the production of *steel.* At the base of the Heliodorus column at Besnagar (Vidisha), datable to *c.* 88 BC, have been found strips of steel (iron with 0.7 per cent carbon), apparently taken from a broken sword that could have been made much earlier. The other find is that of a vase of *brass* (copper, 55 per cent; zinc, 34 per cent; and lead, 3 per cent) from Taxila, datable to the third–second century BC. Unlike steel, brass manufacture seems to have disappeared thereafter, not to be revived until medieval times.

4.5 Extractive Industries

Of the precious **metals,** gold was collected from river-sands; and the five localities (all unidentified) where, according to the *Arthashāstra,* 2.13.3, gold was obtained, were probably those where gold particles were so collected ('transmuted by means of liquids'?). The *Periplus*, Section 63, refers to a 'gold mine' in the Gangetic region (Bengal), which is possibly a misunderstanding that arose from gold being brought there from Assam: in Assam gold used to be collected in the seventeenth century from sands of the northern tributaries of the Brahmaputra. There is, curiously enough, no reference to the gold mines in Karnataka.

Archaeological work in the Zawar mines (Mewar) has established that down to the first century BC, these mines were worked to extract *silver,* though lead and zinc formed associated ores. Apparently, the silver extracted proved uneconomical as mines reached lower levels, and the mines were thereafter not re-opened until the fourteenth century when the metal sought was zinc. The *Arthashāstra*, 2.13.10, mentions a region called 'Kambu' as a source of silver; and if this is a shortened form of Kāmboja, the well-known mines of Panjshīr in Afghanistan, worked until the sixteenth century, might be meant. A silver shortage is possibly indicated by the Kushāns' abandonment of silver coinage altogether.

Copper was profusely used for coinage in our period, but the only mines definitely known to be worked are those of Rajpura Dariba, with a carbon date of AD 185–350. *Lead*, another metal used in Western Satrap and Sātavāhana coinage, probably came from the Zawar and associated mines as long as they were worked for silver.

India is fortunate in having good *iron* ores found near the surface at many places in central India and the peninsula, but the only place where archaeologists have found traces of iron-mining in our period is Adichanallur in southern Tamil Nadu, where the workings are indeed extensive.

Among **precious stones**, India seems to have had two major sources for diamonds. Statements found in the *Arthashāstra* (2.11.37), Ptolemy and the later Tibetan annalist Tārānātha, appear to indicate that the diamond mines of Wairagarh were being worked. The *Arthashāstra*, 7.12.24, also seems to refer to the Deccan diamond mines, and the *Periplus*, Section 56, confirms it by its statement that diamonds were exported from Muziris and other Kerala ports.

From Muziris was also exported beryl (*Periplus*, Section 56), which appears to have been obtained mainly from mines near Coimbatore, Tamil Nadu.

Agate and cornelian exported from Baryaza (Bharuch) (*Periplus*, Section 48) could not have come from 'Ozene' (Ujjain), but from the much nearer Rajpipla mines, whose exploitation goes back to Indus times.

Outside of India, there is Chinese evidence, of *c.* AD 100, for the working of jade mines near Khotan, in Xinjiang, China, just north of the Karakorum range. In the south, Sri Lanka was famous for its 'gems', which presumably meant rubies and sapphires (Pliny; *Periplus*, Section 61; *Arthashāstra*, 2.11.28).

Among the more mundane minerals was **salt**. Strabo, 5.II.6, refers to India's salt mines, and the *Arthashāstra*, 2.15.15, to Saindhava salt; both references suit the Salt-Range salt mines in western Punjab. The Nasik cave inscriptions imply that salt was also collected from saline grounds in villages, for which purpose these used to be dug up.

There was, finally, a major **pearl fishery** on the coast of the Pāṇḍiya kingdom, east of Cape Comorin, in the Gulf of Mannar. Three pearl-fishing spots along this coast are specified in the *Arthashāstra*, 2.11.2; and the *Periplus*, Sections 58 and 59. Khāravela, in his Hathigumpha inscription (*Extract 2.2*), claims to have received pearls in gifts from the Pāṇḍiyan ruler. Both Pliny and the *Periplus*, Section 61, also mention a pearl fishery on the Sri Lankan coast opposite; minor pearl fisheries appear to have existed at two other points on the western coast.

4.6 Artisanal Industries and Transport

This period seems to be mainly marked by the development of a **cotton textile** industry, which, until the British machine-woven cloth dethroned it by the early nineteenth century, was to remain without a rival in the world. It is true that the *Arthashāstra*, 2.11.97–115 (*Extract 4.4*), gives the primary place to wool and animal hair as fibres for apparel, and also speaks of varieties of wild silks. And the *Kāma-sūtra*, 5.5.6 (*Extract 4.2*), mentions not only cotton, but also wool, flax, hemp and even tree-bark out of which village women spun yarn. It is possible that the other coarser fibres still served to clothe the poor; but much for the fine cloth was now being made of cotton. The passage from the *Arthashāstra* itself distinguishes what can only be muslin or varieties of fine cotton (102–106) from ordinary cotton, a reference to which occurs at the end (105) of the passage. Cotton was, therefore, certainly on its way to meet the clothing needs of the rich as well as the poor.

The *Periplus* of the Erythraean Sea (*c.* AD 100) makes a similar distinction between muslin and other cotton fabrics that entered trade in various parts of the country. In the *Arthashāstra*, the region producing muslin (*dukūla*) comprised three different parts of Bengal (Vaṅga, Puṇḍra and Suvarnakuḍya). The *Periplus* too recognizes that the finest muslin (called 'Gangetic', perhaps an allusion to the name *Gangā-jal*, borne by a variety of muslin also in Mug͟hal times) was produced in that region. Other localities which manufactured muslin are identified by the *Periplus* as Ujjain, Gujarat, 'Tagara' (Thair, Maharashtra), coastal Andhra, east Pāṇḍiyan country and Sri Lanka.

According to the *Arthashāstra* (2.11.115), ordinary cotton fabrics of apparently better quality were produced in Bengal, Kalinga, Kāshi (Varanasi), Vatsa (Kausambi), Mathura, Aparānta (Konkan) and Mahish(-mati) on the Narmada. To this list the *Periplus* adds Sind, Gujarat, Ujjain and 'Tagara' (Thair).

India's exports of muslin to the Mediterranean world became an important feature of Indian foreign trade in the first century AD, as we shall see below (*Chapter 4.10*).

The expansion of cotton textile production must have provided employment to large numbers, especially women. Spinning in the absence of the spinning wheel (it did not arrive in India until the

FIGURE 4.4 Pointed cap, Mathura sculpture. R.C. Sharma.

fourteenth century) must have meant exceptionally hard work for the fingers. It seems to have been undertaken exclusively by women, as the *Kāma-sūtra* passage (*Extract 4.2*) confirms. The *Mahājanaka Jātaka* even speaks as if it was women who usually handled the scutch-bow to separate cotton fibres – work that in later times fell mainly to men.

While we are on the subject of textiles, we may note the introduction of a new craft: that of tailoring. Altekar tells us that sewing is referred to in the *Rig-veda* and the *Aitareya Brāhmana*, but Indian clothing as shown in sculpture for both women and men seems to have consisted of a loin-cloth (*dhoti*) tied at the waist and a long piece of cloth thrown over the shoulders. It is with the migrants from the north-west that the tunic and trousers arrive in our period (see the Kanishka statue, *Figure 3.2*); and so also the pointed cap carved in statuary at Mathura (*Figure 4.4*), reminding us of the Sakas of pointed caps in Achaemenid inscriptions and sculpture.

Next to textiles, among crafts, **pottery** employed perhaps the largest number of men and women. In the north, at Taxila and Ahichchhatra, where the pottery of this period has been especially studied, the Northern Black Polished Ware continued to serve the urban market, developing sophisticated forms with spouts, handles and pinched lips. In the south at Arikamedu (near Pondicherry), which may be said to be the type-site for southern pottery, the fabric was coarser and the forms simpler. But it is also the place where a remarkable type of pottery was first studied.

This is called *Rouletted Ware* (*Figure 4.5*). The patterns (bands of dots, decorative lines, closely put cross-lines, etc.) of the ware appear to have originated in the Mediterranean world, but the pottery itself is

FIGURE 4.5 Rouletted Ware fragments from Arikamedu. R.E.H. Wheeler, *et al.*

not found there. It has now been found at many places in India (see *Map 4.1*), and also outside India, in Sri Lanka and even Bali in Indonesia. In the first and second centuries AD, it is likely to have been manufactured in some localities within India, presumably by pressing rotatable discs (roulettes), with banded patterns on their thick sides, against rotating pots. The roulettes themselves have not been found and so no workshop or manufacturing locality has, in fact, been traced.

Another sector which employed a number of persons was the **building** industry. In a place like Taxila, close to the hills, stone and rubble provided the main building material, but in other places bricks were used instead: these were thin, and rather long and broad. In Arikamedu, for example, the bricks were only 6.4 to 7.4 cm thick, while they were 35.4 to 38.10 cm long, and about 21 cm or 27 cm broad. The use of large stone blocks to raise large structures had still not begun on any scale, but *rock-cut* caves, as at Nasik, Kanheri and Karle, exhibited new skills in stone-cutting. This extended to stone statuary, as at Bharhut, Sanchi and Mathura, and in Gandhāra, where not only skill but

Map 4.1 India: Products, Routes, Marts, Ports

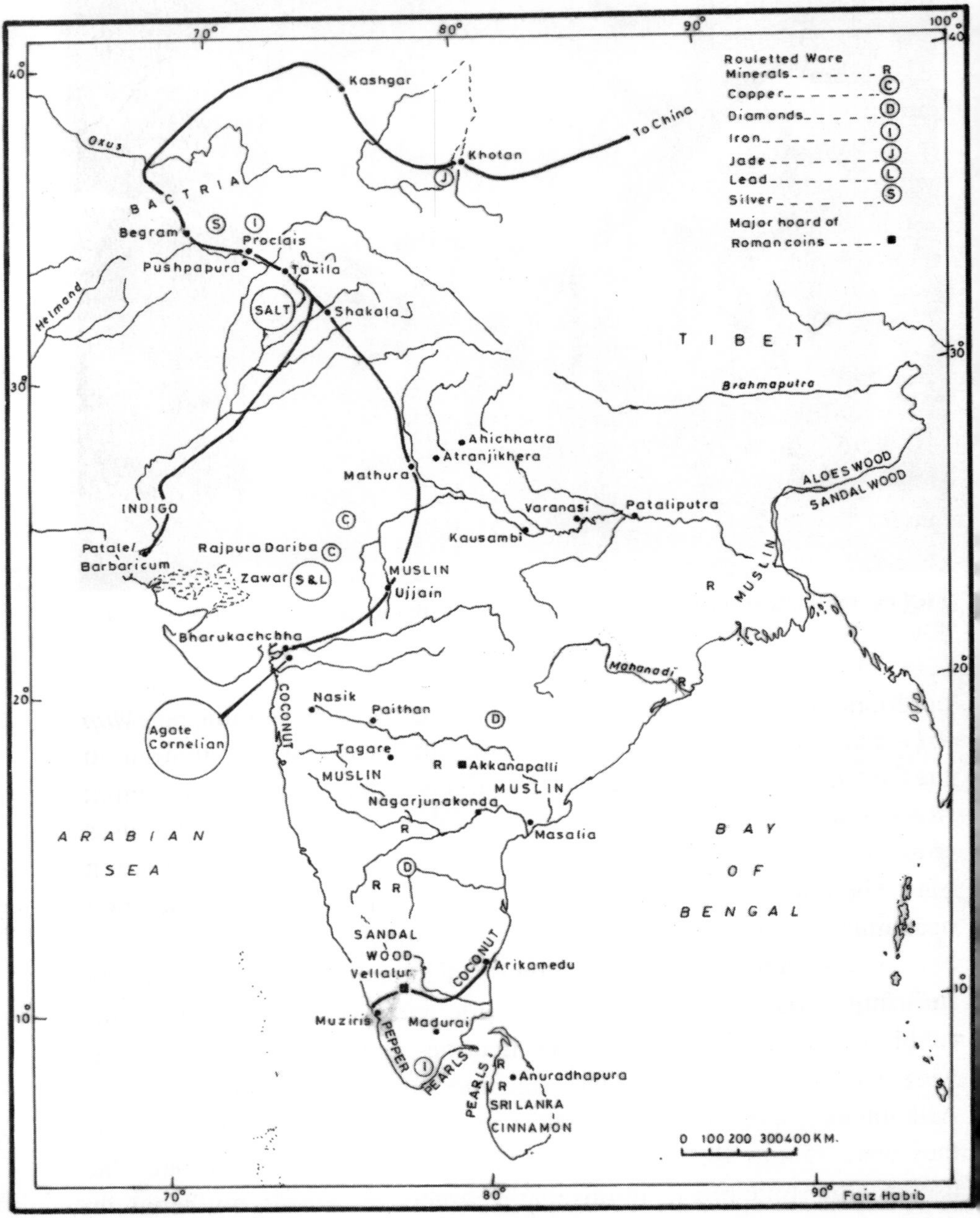

much hard labour, given the tools of the time, was also required, from quarrying to cutting and shaping.

Among **minor crafts** may be mentioned the *glass bead* industry. Glass beads were found in profusion in Taxila; and from south India comes the report of a manufacturing centre in first–third centuries AD at Porunthal, Dindugul district, Tamil Nadu, where the industrial waste found was estimated to contain about a million glass beads. Marshall, in his report on Taxila, however, doubts if any of the glass-ware (bowls, etc.) found there in rather small quantity was of local manufacture.

Jewellery must have employed some very skilled workmen. The main evidence of gold-work comes from Tilla-tepe in north Afghanistan where over 20,000 gold objects dating to the first century AD were found. The gold was splendid, and there are signs of Hellenistic skill, but the art of the local craftsmen was still of a modest quality.

On **transport,** our major source is sculpture. A sculptured panel from Mathura (*Figure 4.6*) pictures three ways of conveyance, viz. horse-back, elephant, and a two-wheel wooden ox-drawn wagon with windows. The horses are without convex saddle and horse-bit, being controlled through nose-band. One horse already figured (*Figure 3.4*) has a rope-like toe-stirrup, the other two lack it. Ox-drawn wagons similar to those shown here are depicted in another sculptured archway, where a pair of horses is also shown drawing the same kind of wagon; without the horse-collar, the strain on horses' necks and windpipes must have been very severe. The other side of the same archway shows an open cart drawn by a horse (*Figure 4.7*) – a type still to be seen on Indian rural roads today.

These sculptures at a Jain stupa at Mathura probably picture the conveyances used by visitors to the holy site, and so illustrate urban

FIGURE 4.6 Town conveyances, Mathura sculpture. V.A. Smith.

FIGURE 4.7 Open horse-drawn wagon (middle row), Mathura sculpture.
V.A. Smith.

conveyances rather than means of long-distance transport. The dromedary (one-humped camel) had not yet arrived, so that we must imagine that bullock-carts and pack-oxen, besides river-boats, must have carried the bulk of long-distance traffic.

4.7 Towns and Commercial Organization

It is supposed by some historians, notably R.S. Sharma, that there was a surge towards urbanization, i.e. an increase in the numbers of towns and enlargement of their individual sizes, during this period. However, we have no population statistics to build any thesis upon, and archaeological work on historical town-sites has been also quite patchy and fragmented. Taxila, the only great urban site to have been extensively excavated, has certainly a story to tell that supports R.S. Sharma's hypothesis; but, after all, it is the story of only one town. The Bhir mound, which contained the main city in Mauryan times, was about 1.1 km long and 670 metres broad. This was abandoned for a larger city (Sirkap), planned on a 'chess-board' pattern (with streets meeting each other at right angles), suggestive of tight municipal control. Its precise inhabited area is not stated, but the wall surrounding the city is said to be 5.6 km long. Under the Kushāns, another city (Sirsukh) on a planned pattern was built alongside Sirkap; it formed a rectangle, 1.37 km long and 1 km broad, protected by a fortified wall.

Mathura, which, to judge from its inscriptions, was one of the Kushān capitals, has had its remains so overlaid by subsequent occupation that no estimate of its ancient size can be hazarded. But at two other sites, Ahichchhatra and Atranjikhera (both in western Uttar Pradesh), the ruins still remain within open land. The mounds of the first lie within a perimeter of 5.6 km, while the ruins of the other stretch to a length of over 1.1 km and have a width of 0.4 km. Kausambi, known to be a major town on the Yamuna near Allahabad, had ramparts with a peripheral circuit of 6.4 km. It is, however, not certain if the entire area within these ramparts was fully occupied.

In the Deccan, archaeological work undertaken at and around the Ikhāku capital, Nagarjunakonda, on the Krishna river, before its submergence in the Nagarjunasagar lake, disclosed a citadel wall enclosing an irregular rectangle approximately 1 km by 0.6 km. The actual urban area might, however, have been larger.

Many towns are mentioned in Greek sources, notably the *Periplus* and Ptolemy, as political centres, marts and ports, but there is little indication of their size. Larger towns drew religious establishments, whether Buddhist, Brahmanical or Jain, to their vicinity, as one can see particularly at Taxila, Mathura, Nagarjunakonda and Madurai. Such towns also encouraged the establishment of satellite settlements, which might have arisen partly due to the pull of the markets (for agricultural produce or crafts) in the main city. Sites of inscriptions around Taxila, Mathura and Madurai (*Maps 4.2 a, b, c*) offer reasonable evidence for such satellite settlements.

It hardly admits of doubt that the population of the towns displayed a far more complex structure than the villages, and the distances between the upper and lower levels were here far greater. There was, to begin with, a large mass of attendants and slaves. In Mathura sculpture, we see a rich woman standing erect, fanned by a woman attendant, while another holds a sun-shade over her and yet another carries a garland (*Figure 4.8*). Grooms run ahead of their master's horses (*Figure 4.6*). There were also 'professionals' like musicians and dancers, as depicted in yet another Mathura sculpture (*Figure 4.9).* The town artisans and merchants appear in various inscriptions and we will presently discuss their mutual relationships. The *Kāmasūtra* has sketched for us the ways of the *nāgaraka,* 'townsman', a middle-class idler subsisting on varied sources of income, and dabbling in polite culture and casual dalliances. Finally, the aristocracy into whose harem

FIGURE 4.8 Woman with three women attendants, Mathura sculpture. This bears an inscription of *mahākshatrapa* Sodasa, late 1st century BC. V.A. Smith.

FIGURE 4.9 Musicians and dancers, Mathura sculpture. V.A. Smith.

the Mathura sculpture takes us (*Figure 4.10*), where, perhaps, we have a rare glimpse of the eunuch-slave: misery and luxury stood side by side here.

It seems likely that both commerce and crafts in the towns were controlled by caste corporations called *shreṇi,* a term which is usually rendered as 'guild'. The term makes its appearance in the inscriptions of the first and second centuries AD. Its earliest occurrence is perhaps in an inscription of U<u>sh</u>avadāta, the Shaka prince, in the Nasik caves (*Extract 4.5A*), *c.* AD 100, which records the entrusting of two sums of money to two *shreṇis* of the town of Govardhana, both *shreṇis* being those of weavers (*kolikanika*). The *shreṇis* were to provide, out of the interest due on the entrusted money, the costs of clothing, etc., for a set of twenty monks of the *Saṁgha*. The implication is that the weavers' *shreṇis* themselves would lend out the funds at interest to obtain the necessary income. In a later Nasik inscription (third century), a Shaka woman records an endowment for providing medicines to Buddhist monks by placing different sums of money with the *shreṇis* of potters (*kularika*), noria makers (*odayaṁtrika*) and oil-millers (*tilapi<u>sh</u>aka*). Two inscriptions from Junnar nearby mention endowments placed with guilds of 'Koṇāchika' (?) and of bamboo workers. A similar endowment is recorded in an inscription of Huvi<u>sh</u>ka's time (year 28 = *c.* AD 188) (*Extract 4.5B*): here, for the purpose of daily feeding a hundred Brahmans, an official entrusted

FIGURE 4.10 Harem scenes: toilet of a rich woman, Mathura sculpture. R.C. Sharma.

MAP 4.2 Towns and Satellite Settlements: (a) Taxila, (b) Mathura, (c) Madurai

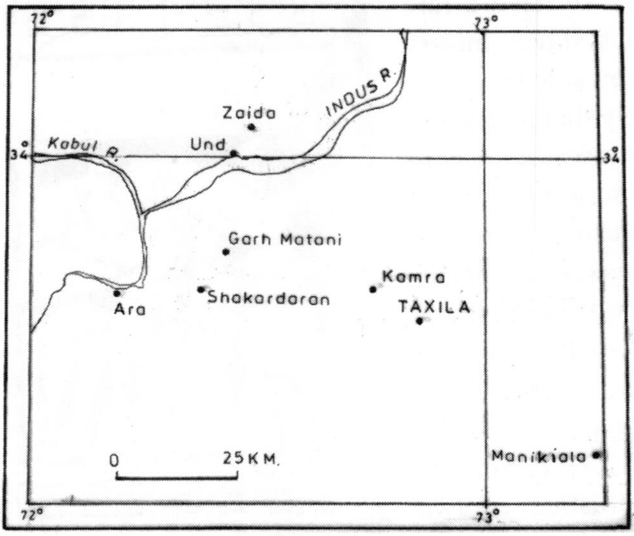

(a) Kushān Inscriptions near Taxila

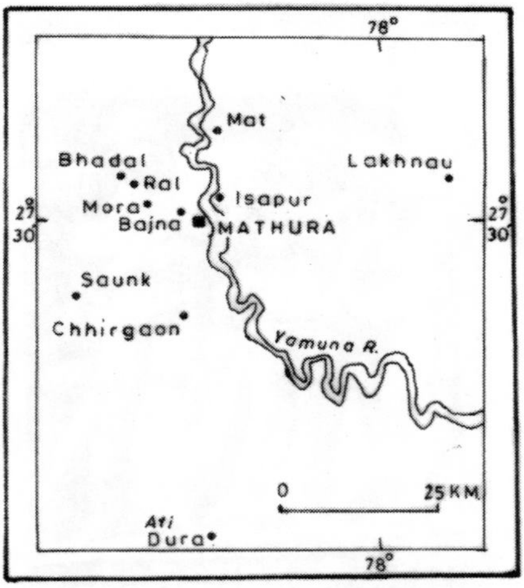

(b) Kushān Inscriptions near Mathura

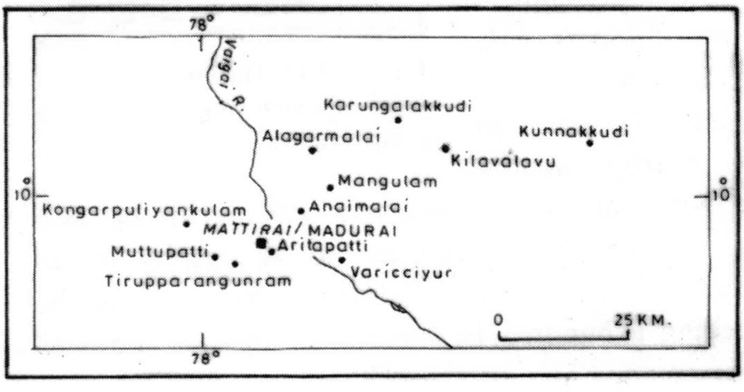

(c) Tamil-Brāhmī Inscriptions near Madurai

money to two *shreṇis*, one that of flour makers (*samitakara*), the other of a profession whose name is illegible. A fourth inscription of this kind comes from Nagarjunakonda (AD 333?), which is in a damaged condition, but gives us the record of money entrusted with *senis* (*shreṇis*) of betel-leaf sellers (*panika*) and confectioners (*pavika*) among others, so as to yield monthly interest to be spent on the embellishments of a temple.

From these inscriptions one may well imagine the presence in the towns of quite prosperous artisans organized in wealthy guilds. But the reality is likely to have been different. *Shreṇis* were probably not bodies of ordinary artisans at all, but of their employers or merchant-masters. In a central Indian inscription (Bandogarh, Madhya Pradesh), of the year 51 (*c.* AD 211), a *goṭhi* (Sanskrit *goshṭhi*) comprising four merchants (*negama*), two traders (*vanijaka*), one goldsmith (*suvanakara*), one carpenter-cum-blacksmith (*kāṭhikārika-kamāra*), all duly named, is credited with the excavation of a cave. Now it is clear that the same person could not have combined in himself the totally diverse professions of carpenter and blacksmith. He was presumably, like the others, a merchant, but one who dealt especially with carpenters and blacksmiths, employing them or buying their products. At Kausambi, in an inscription of year 81 (*c.* AD 241), the *shreṇi* of stone-masons (*pastharika*) claims to have installed certain stone-seats, and this could be a real guild of working stone-masons – but could as easily, of course, be of their employers.

The inference that persons who composed the *shreṇis* were actually contractors, or merchants and not artisans themselves, is confirmed by three passages in the *Arthashāstra*. In one (2.4.16), after specifying in which quarters of the town various categories of artisans and other workers ought to live, it allots a separate space for 'foreign merchants and (members of ?) *shreṇis*'. In the other two passages (4.1.2, 3) it is stated that if one wished to get some work done on material at hand, one needed to approach a *kārushāsitaraḥ* (that is, an employer of artisans), or a trusted intermediary or a *svavittakāravaḥ*, an artisan working on his own but, in the last case, only with an assurance (*pramāṇā*) from the *shreṇi*. If the artisan died, the *shreṇi* was to assure the return of the material that had been given out. One can deduce from this that the *shreṇis* were in fact instruments in the hands of masters or merchants for control over the artisans, whether by the force of its laws or customs (mentioned in *Manusmriti*, VIII.41) or by the ties of usury, from which, as five inscriptions from our period so clearly imply, the *shreṇis* derived at least part of their income.

One other matter on which we should like to know more is the relationship between the state and the city. By building ramparts around several cities, as archaeology bears witness to, the state undoubtedly provided a certain amount of security to the towns. What it took from the cities in the form of taxes and other impositions is not, however, clear. Inscriptions of the time tell us next to nothing about their magnitude. The *Arthashāstra*, chapters 2.21 and 2.22, prescribes that tolls should be levied strictly at the city-gates; and that on the merchandise entering the city, one-fifth of the price should be paid. The tax was to be one-sixth of the price on perishable material like flowers, fruits, vegetables, etc. Far lower duties (one-tenth to one-twentieth) on various articles of merchandise, of both high and low values, are also prescribed. Apparently, for better collection of tax, the *Arthashāstra* states that no sales should be permitted outside the city at the actual local sites of production, but that the sales should occur only in the city. The *Manusmriti* prescribes no rates of tolls, but urges moderation. It allows (VII.137–38) the ruler to levy an annual tax on common merchants, and to demand one day of unpaid labour per month from artisans and *shūdras* who live by labour. We may recall that such imposition of forced labour (*vishṭi*) appears as a ruler's prerogative in Rudradāman's Junagadh inscription of AD 150.

4.8 Money and Credit

During the five hundred years (200 BC – AD 300) we deal with in this monograph, punch-marked coins that had originated in a non-literate age were steadily replaced by coins in gold, silver and copper (and additionally in cupro-nickel and lead) carrying the sovereigns' busts with legends proclaiming their names and titles. The early coins issued by the Greek rulers were in gold, silver and copper; but gold-minting was abandoned early in the second century BC, and so the Greek gold coins ('staters') of the Attic standard (8.55 grammes) probably never came into use in India. The silver coins ('drachmas'), also of the Attic standard, weighing 4.87 grammes, were issued for

Bactria, while for the Indian possessions the Greek rulers and their successors in the north-west minted silver coins weighing 3.75 grammes. The Western Satraps, however, issued silver coins weighing no more than 2.33 grammes. The Kushāns, from Vima Kadphises onwards, abandoned the minting of silver, and issued only gold and copper coinage. Their gold coins imitated the Roman aurei and weighed 8.03 grammes each.

In the peninsula the Sātavāhanas issued very few silver coins, and these followed the weight standard of the Western Satraps' issues. The Sātavāhanas mostly minted in potin, lead and copper with widely ranging weights. In the precious metals, gold and silver, south India went over practically to Roman coins from about the beginning of the Christian era. The Roman gold coin *aureus* weighed 10.08 grammes under Augustus (d. AD 14), but under Nero (AD 54–68), its weight was reduced to 8.06 grammes, a standard that the Kushāns followed for their gold coinage. Its import into India ceased after Caracalla devalued it by 20 per cent in 214. The silver coin of the Roman empire was *denarius*, in which the silver content was first reduced by Nero in AD 64 and then substantially by Trajan (98–117).

Coins did not indicate their denominations in their legends. Ushavadāta's Nasik cave inscription of *c.* AD 100 (*Extract 4.5A*) uses the term *kāhāpaṇa* or *kārshāpana*, for the silver coin issued by Nahapāṇa to a standard of 2.33 grammes; and it then gives the value of one *suvarṇa*, or gold coin, as 35 *kārshāpanas*. Since, according to the *Periplus*, Section 49, Roman coins in gold and silver sold for profit at Barygaza (Bharuch) at this time, and since Nahapāna issued no gold coin himself, Ushavadāta must by *suvarṇa* mean the Roman *aureus* of 8.06 grammes. This gives us a gold–silver ratio of 1:10.1, which seems quite reasonable. In the Mathura inscription of year 28 in Huvishka's reign, two monetary endowments are made in terms of *purāṇas*, or 'old coins' (*Extract 4.5B*). These could mean either the silver coins issued prior to Kadphises II, who had ceased minting them, or, which is less likely, the punch-marked silver coins that too had by now ceased to be minted. In either case, it accords with the mention of *purāṇa* as a silver coin in the *Manusmriti* (VIII.136). While the *Arthashāstra*, 2.12.24, treats *paṇa* as a silver coin, the *Manusmriti* treats *kārshāpaṇa* as a copper one. This may mean that after the cessation of silver coinage by the Kushāns, the name of the silver piece was transferred to their copper issues.

The two inscriptions which we have reproduced in *Extracts 4.5A* and *B* are also important for the information they yield on conditions of credit. The Mathura inscription of *c.* 188 tells us that interest (*vriddhi*) was paid month by month (*mās-ānumasaṁ*), while the Nasik inscription of *c.* 100 gives two rates of interest (*vadhi*), viz. 1 per cent and 0.75 per cent. Assuming that these are monthly rates, we get annual rates of 12 and 9 per cent without compounding. In an inflation-free economy these would be very high rates, though in the context of arrangements made with the *shreṇis* or guilds, these must have been regarded at that time as rather conservative or moderate returns on a usurious investment. The actual rates at which the *shreṇis* lent must have been much higher.

4.9 Inland and Overland Trade

Every town that contained non-agricultural populations had to obtain food-stuffs for consumption and raw material for manufacture from the countryside. In so far as the state or landed aristocracy living in towns collected taxes or rents from villages, whether in money or in kind, and spent the resources so gathered in the towns, the local trade was in one direction, i.e. from villages to towns. Villages sold grain in order to pay tax or rent in money, or gave over part of the produce to the tax or rent collector. In either case, a large part of the products was sold and consumed in the towns. Such trade is often called *induced* trade. Villages themselves depended on the towns for very little, their 'imports' comprising some iron tools or salt (then an expensive commodity in some parts of the country). But in some rural areas there were specialized crops or products, notably varieties of cotton, sugarcane or indigo, pepper, wild silks, etc., which had markets beyond the neighbouring towns. In our period, as we have seen, muslin began to be manufactured in certain regions, which was then exported to distant markets. Similar could be the case with rouletted ware. The *Arthashāstra*, 7.12–24, speaks of diamonds from the south as valuable articles of commerce; and Khāravela, ruler of Kalinga, obviously greatly valued pearls from fisheries on the Pāṇḍiyan coasts (*Extract 2.2*).

The routes along which these goods were transported can

only be vaguely determined by connecting the major towns, as on our *Map 4.1*. The *Periplus* of the Erythraean Sea, Sections 39, 48 and 56, implies that the ports of Barbaricum (in the Indus delta) and Barygaza (Bharuch) obtained commercial goods from Bactria and Proclais (Pushkalavati or Charsadda near Peshawar). Ujjain ('Ozene') was apparently an important mart in Bharuch's hinterland (*Periplus*, Section 48), while the finds of Roman coins in the Coimbatore gap suggests that a major commercial route ran through it connecting the port of Muziris (Muchiripattanam or Cranganore) with the Tamil Nadu plains.

A major event on India's north-western borders was undoubtedly the opening of the 'Great Silk Road' to China. When Alexander and his troops crossed the Oxus in the 320s BC, they were never made aware of the existence of China and of the routes leading to it from Central Asia. But in the quest of jade, which was highly prized in China, Chinese trade with Khotan (Xinjiang), famous for its jade mines, was established well before AD 100, when the jade mines are noticed in the *Chhien Hanshu*. In return, China had true silk (mulberry silk) and lacquer ware to offer, commodities that, as Szuma Chien had noted about two hundred years earlier (91 BC), countries west of Xinjiang lacked. Chinese silk, in particular, gained a practically universal market by the first century AD among the rich of Parthian Iran, the Roman empire and probably also India – though in India the possibility of confusion with wild silks makes much evidence for silk untrustworthy. The demand opened the 'Silk Road', passing through Bactria and Iran, or alternatively (especially if wars closed the route *via* Iran) through Bactria on to Bharuch and over the Arabian Sea. The newly opened commerce may be partly responsible for the abundance of gold at Tilla Tepe, and the presence of Roman artefacts and Chinese lacquerware at Begram, dated to late first century BC and first century AD (see *Chapter 3.1*). The ability of the Kushān emperors to shift to gold coinage on the Roman imperial standard also probably owed much to revenue derived from this trade.

4.10 Trans-Oceanic Trade

In India it must have always been observed, especially on or near the coasts, that in the summer months winds blow from the south-

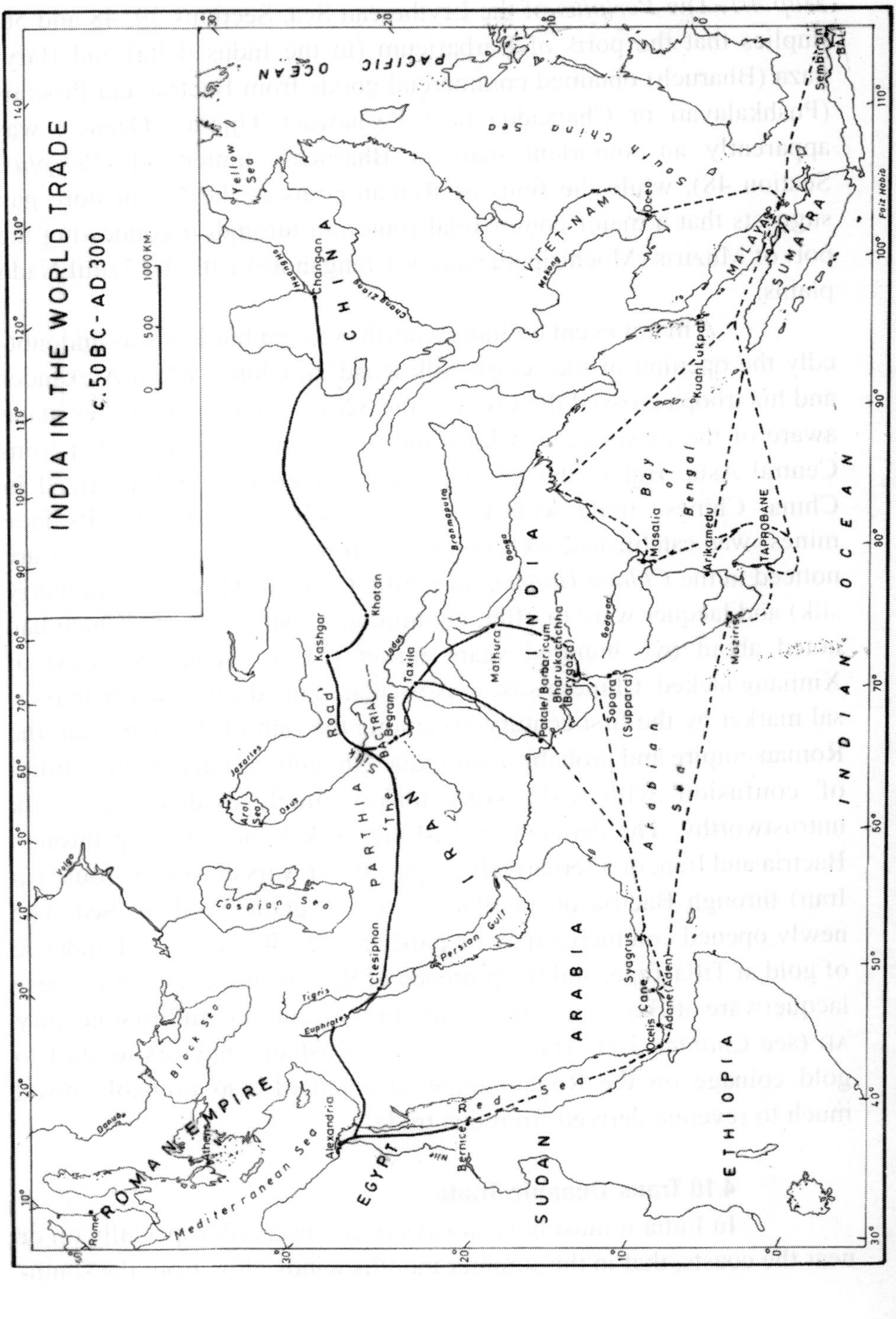

MAP 4.3 India in the World Trade

west over the sea, bringing the main season of the rains, and that the winds turn in the opposite direction, blowing from the north-east from land to the sea in winter, bringing about a fresh rainy season in parts of south India and Sri Lanka (after the winds cross the Bay of Bengal). These winds are respectively called the South-west and North-east '**Monsoons**' (the word 'monsoon' being a corruption, apparently, of the Arabic word *mausam*, season). It is probable that when sailing vessels in early times moved along the coasts, they took advantage of the knowledge that the monsoon winds would blow in a particular direction and arranged their voyages accordingly. Nearchus, Alexander's admiral, made his voyage from the Indus delta to the Persian Gulf in the winter of 324–25 BC, aided doubtless by the North-east Monsoon. He sailed close to the coast; and there was as yet no comprehension that vessels could go far out into what we now call the Arabian Sea. Even when, in *c.* 118, Eudox of Cyzicus made voyages to India from Egypt with an Indian survivor from a ship-wreck as his guide (as reported by Strabo), it is not clear that any new trading route had been discovered: the shore-line could merely have been followed up to the Gulf of Oman.

It was around the end of the first century BC that a radical change occurred in Arabian Sea navigation. A geographical perception of the configuration of the Arabian Sea was formed, with the central notion of the Indian peninsula jutting into the Indian Ocean and crossing the same lines of latitude as those of the southern end of the Red Sea in the west. The accounts of this comprehension and of its use for navigation are not given in any Indian source, but solely in a Latin text (Pliny's *Natural History*) and a Greek trade manual (*Periplus* of the Erythraean sea), both written in the first century AD. The relevant passages are given in our *Extracts 4.6 A* and *B*).

The **new discovery** essentially consisted in this: if sailing vessels made use of the summer and winter monsoons, they could directly cross and recross the Erythraean Sea (Arabian Sea), immensely shortening the distance traversed between India's western coast and the ports at the southern end of the Red Sea. Hypalus or Hippalus was the name given to the aiding wind, the South-west Monsoon; and the *Periplus* inserts the legend that Hippalus was actually the mariner who first made the open sea voyages with the aid of this wind. Since commercial sailings could never be kept a secret, not only the Greek merchants who came to Red Sea ports from Egypt, but also Arabs, Indian and Iranians, all took advantage of the discovery, by whomsoever made.

We must, therefore, expect a great expansion of navigational activity to have taken place by the end of the first century BC. Strabo, who visited Egypt in 27–24 BC, wrote that by his time 'up to a hundred and twenty ships make their way under sail from Myos Hormos [Egyptian port at the northern end of the Red Sea] for India, whereas previously under the Ptolemies [whose rule ended in 30 BC], very few people dared to launch their ships and trade in Indian goods.' Obviously, the shortening of the sea-routes had this effect. Not only did the number of ships increase, but the ships themselves had to be larger in order to carry more supplies and more cargo, since they would be far away from any shores for so many days, and could make only a single onward and return voyage during the year. Indeed, the *Periplus*, Section 36, mentions Indian merchants of Barygaza (Bharuch) as sending cargo in 'big vessels' to Persia. While Greek and Roman ships, built in the Mediterranean, were strongly structured with nailed timbers, the *Periplus* refers to local rafts on the African coast and Oman as being 'sewn' boats, i.e. with their timbers stitched together by rope. Although it does not tell us how Indian sea-going vessels were built, India in later times (almost until the sixteenth century) had ships built with coir-sewn timbers without use of iron nails; and this might well have been the case in the first century AD, the fibre being possibly different (e.g. hemp). However built, it may be assumed that not only did Indian ships obtain a larger size, they also multiplied in numbers to take advantage of the newly opened sea-routes away from the shores.

As to the Arabian Sea sailings, the shift to open-sea voyages probably occurred only in stages, as Warmington has suggested (*Map 4.3*). First, the usual terminal port of the coastal trade, namely the main port in the Indus delta, called by the Greeks 'Barbaricum', was connected directly with Arabian ports on or near the Red Sea. In the next stage, voyages were directly made to the latter port from Barygaza (Bharuch) at the head of the Gulf of Cambay and Indian ports further south such as 'Sigerus' (unidentified). Finally, despite the voyages involving a turn away from the main directions of the wind for quite a distance, direct voyages between the Red Sea and south Indian ports (notably, Muziris) and Sri Lanka began to be undertaken. All of this had been apparently well established by the middle of the first century AD, if not even earlier. Archaeology, through the finds of early imperial Roman coins and artefacts in southern India, confirms what the Greek and Latin texts tell us.

The shorter sea voyages and the larger amount of shipping, both made possible an enormous increase in the volume of trade between India and the Mediterranean world. Goods from India were received at the Egyptian ports on the Red Sea and taken across land to Alexandria from where they were diffused over the Roman empire across the Mediterranean; Roman goods flowed similarly in the reverse direction.

It is fortunate for us that the anonymous author of the *Periplus,* an Egyptian Greek merchant, has described, from his own direct observation, the major articles involved in the trade. Among India's major items of export were round or black pepper, exported from the south Indian ports, and long pepper, grown in eastern India and exported from Barygaza (Bharuch). Round pepper was exported in such large quantities to the Roman empire that it became cheaper there than long pepper, reversing their relative prices in India. Another spice exported in considerable quantities from Muziris was cinnamon ('malabathron'). True cinnamon is a product of Sri Lanka, whose earliest name, Taṁraparni ('Taprobane' in Greek), meant 'land of the copper-coloured leaf', i.e. cinnamon; and cinnamon must therefore have been largely a re-export from Muziris, which received it from Sri Lanka.

Pearls fished off the Paṇḍiyan coast (today's Gulf of Tuticorin), as well as off the opposite Sri Lanka coast, were highly prized at Rome and were deemed superior to those obtained from the Persian Gulf. Besides exporting these pearls, Muziris and other Malabar ports exported diamonds, which must have come from the 'Golkunda' mines, as well as beryl, brought from the Coimbatore mines. Barbaricum, at the mouth of the Indus, exported turquoise (source unknown) and lapis lazuli (which must have come from Badakhshan). Barygaza (Bharuch) exported onyx and agate (from the neighbouring Rajpipla mines), and ivory. Different kinds of drugs and resins formed other items of export from this port.

Finally, textile exports were assuming increasing importance. Bengal exported muslin, and Barbaricum and Barygaza, cotton goods and yarn. Barbaricum also exported indigo. Chinese pelts exported from Barbaricum and Chinese silk from Barygaza had probably reached these ports by the land-routes. But Chinese silk, exported from Muziris, must have been brought to that port from China by the sea-route, and this provides a strong hint that India's oceanic commerce with China had now been opened.

The merchandise that India received as **imports** from the west included coral, a greatly favoured item in India. Among manufactures, linen cloth, both plain and multi-coloured, was imported, as also glass and glassware. Among minerals, realgar (arsenic) and antimony were imported; Muziris also provided a market for copper, tin and lead, for Indian mines of these metals lay in the north and transport by sea could have been cheaper. Mediterranean wines were also shipped to India, and finds of Roman amphoras at archaeological sites bear witness to this commerce. For the royal or aristocratic classes, slave-musicians and slave-girls for concubinage were also recognized as suitable import items, specifically at Bharuch.

Above all, it was **the Roman money**, both gold and silver, which would always bring profit at all the major ports: Barbaricum, Barygaza and Muziris. Their heavy import is confirmed by the finds of over 6,000 coins, mainly of gold and silver, but also copper, at various sites in the Indian peninsula, besides a large number in Sri Lanka (see *Map 4.5*). Roman coins could have been in demand in India due to the advantage they provided as a standard currency in all the three metals. But their heavy imports could also represent payment against a constant net export surplus that India built up, and which could only be paid for by a drain of coin and bullion from the Roman empire. This drain, Pliny (d. AD 70) estimated at not less than 50 million sisterces or 12.5 million silver denarii a year (*Extract 4.6A*); and, for that reason, he looked at the whole trade with a censorious eye. Indeed, from emperor Tiberius (AD 14–37) onwards, there follows a stream of condemnations at Rome of the heavy expenditure by the rich and powerful on such expensive articles as Chinese silk, Indian pearls, gems, muslin, pepper, perfumes and other luxuries. Characteristically, one of the critics, the philosopher

Seneca (4 BC – AD 65), himself owned five hundred tables with legs of ivory!

There is no direct account of the use of monsoon winds for voyages across the Bay of Bengal, but that this began practically simultaneously with similar developments over the Arabian Sea is implied by the evidence we have of both trade, and early Indian settlements and principalities in **South-east Asia**. In distant Vietnam, at the ancient port of Oc-éo in the Mekong delta, have been found seals and rings with Brāhmī inscriptions, as well as Roman medallions, of the second century AD, and the oldest Sanskrit inscription of the area, mentioning an Indian or Indianized ruler Shrī Māra, found at Vo-Canh, belongs to the second or third century AD. In southern Thailand, on the Bay of Bengal coast, at Kuan Lukpat has been found an oval stone seal bearing northern Brāhmī characters of first–third centuries AD. Rouletted ware has been found at Sembiran in Bali, Indonesia, which must have been imported from south India in the first or second century AD. An actual narrative of a 90-day voyage in an Indian vessel from Sri Lanka directly to Sumatra or Java, undertaken *c.* 413, is given by the Chinese pilgrim Fahien, with a sense of all the terrors that a bottomless, shoreless ocean could inspire. To sail with the monsoons was not a task for the faint-hearted, but Fahien was accompanied by a large body of Indian merchants, not otherwise known for bravery.

While the commercial contacts established with South-east Asia in the early Christian centuries subsequently spawned Indian Sanskrit-using principalities in Indonesia, Malaya, Cambodia and Vietnam, it is likely that India otherwise also gained much from the connection. One consequence could have been the import of coconut saplings from the tree's original habitats in South-east Asia, which plant, as we have seen early in this chapter (*4.1*) now spread over large parts of the country's coastal areas, providing India with a lasting economic asset.

TABLE 4.1 Chronology

	BC
Opening of Silk Route to China	*c.* 100
Beginning of direct voyages across Arabian Sea	*c.* 50
	AD
Nero's reform of Roman coinage	64
First epigraphic reference to coconut and to *shreṇi*	*c.* 100
Periplus of Erythraean Sea compiled before	106
Kushans begin issue of gold coinage	*c.* 120
Sudarshana lake, Junagadh, breached and repaired	150

Extract 4.1

Classes in a Village*: Milindapañho*

[Nāgasena answers King Milinda:] Suppose, O King, that in some village, the 'lord of the village' (*gāmasāmika*) were to order the crier (*āṇāpaka*), saying: 'Go, crier, bring all the villagers *(gāmikā)* quickly together before me.' And he, in obedience to that order, were to stand in the midst of the village and were thrice to call out: 'Let all the villagers assemble at once in the presence of the lord!' And they should assemble in haste, and have an announcement made to the 'lord of the village', saying: 'All the villagers, sire, have assembled. Do now whatsoever you require.' Now when the 'lord of the village', O King, is summoning all the 'men-of-houses' (*kuṭipurise*), he issues orders to all the villagers. But it is not they who assemble in obedience to his order; it is the 'men of houses'. And the lord is satisfied therewith, knowing that such is the number of his villagers. There are many others who do not come – women and men, women slaves (*dāsī*) and men slaves (*dāsa*), hired workmen (*bhatakā*), servants (*kammakarā*), [ordinary] villagers (*gāmikā*), sick people (*gilānā*), oxen, buffalo, sheep, goats and dogs – but all these do not count. It was (only) with reference to the heads of houses that the order was issued in the words: 'Let all assemble.'

Note: Translation by T.W. Rhys Davids, *Questions of Milinda*, I, Oxford, 1890, pp. 208–09, slightly modified after comparison with published text, *Milindapañho*, ed. V. Trenckner, London, 1880/1962, p. 167.

Extract 4.2
Rural Women Labourers and their Oppressors: Vātsāyana, Kāmasūtra, 5.5.5 and 6

5. A young village-headman (*grāmādhipati*), official (*āyukta*) and son of a plough-owner (*halotthavṛitti*) can approach village women by mere word. These women are called approachable women (*charshaṇi*) by the men of pleasure (*viṭa*).

6. With these women union can be attained on many occasions, namely, when they render forced labour (*vishṭikarma*), when they enter the (store-)house, when they bring material in or take it out, when they repair/clean the house, when they work on the fields (*kshetrakarma*), and when they take cotton, wool, flax, hemp and tree-bark and bring in return the yarn, and in the course of selling, buying and exchanging various articles, and on other occasions.

Note: Translation of passage owed to Professor Sreeramula R. Sarma.

Extract 4.3
Service Tenures and a *Gahapati's* Reservoir: Myakadoni Inscription, Bellary district, Karnataka

Success! Of the Sātavahana king *(raño),* Siri—Pulumāvi, the first day of the first (fortnight) of the second month of winter in the eighth year, in the *mahāsenāpati* Khaṁdanāka's *janapada*, the *(a)hāra* of Sātavāhani, the *(gu)mika* (captain?) Kumāradata's village Vepuraka, wherein resident, the *gahapati* (house-head), Koṁta (by tribe?), Sambe, dug this reservoir (*talaka*).

Note: The inscription (text and translation) was published by V.S. Sukthankar in *Epigraphia Indica*, XIV, pp. 153–55. Our rendering follows the substance of his translation, but the contents have been re-arranged to correspond closely to the original Prakrit text.

Extract 4.4
The Textile Products of India: *Arthashāstra*, 2.11.97–115
[WOOL]

97. Woollen cloth is undyed, fully dyed and half-dyed, with threads laid in the needle, variegated in weaving, with pieces joined together and with broken-off threads. **98.** The blanket, the *kauchapaka* [covering], the *kulamitikā* and *saumitikā* [housings for elephants], the horse's saddle-cloth, the coloured blanket, the *talichchhaka*, the armour [?], *paristoma* [kind of blanket] and the *samantabhadraka* [belt or hem inside of armour] are (varieties of) woollen cloth. **99.** Slippery and wet, as it were, fine and soft is best. **100.** The black *bhiṅgisī*, made of a collection of eight woollen strands (and) the [cloth called] *apasāraka*, which keeps off rain – that is (woollen cloth) from Nepāla. **101.** The *sampuṭikā*, the *chaturashikā*, the *lambarā*, the *kaṭavānaka*, the *pravāraka* and the *sattalikā* are (products from) the hair of animals.

[MUSLIN]

102. The *dukūla* [muslin] from the Vaṅgas [Bengal] is white and smooth. **103.** That from Puṇḍras [north Bangladesh] is dark and smooth like a gem. **104.** That from Suvarṇa-kudya [west Bengal] is of the colour of the sun, with gem-smooth water-weave, with a uniform weave and with a mixed weave. **105.** Of these there is cloth with a single yarn, or with one and a half yarns, or with two or three or four yarns [in the warp and weft]. **106.** By that is explained the *kshauma* from Kāshi and the Puṇḍras.

[WILD SILKS]

107. The *patrorṇa*-silk [*patrorṇa*, 'wool in the leaf'] comes from the Magadhas, the Puṇḍras and Suvarṇakuḍya. **108.** The *nāga*-tree, the *likucha,* the *bakula* and the banyan tree are the sources. **109.** That from the *nāga*-tree is yellow. **110.** That from the *likucha* is wheat-coloured. **111.** That from the *bakula* is white. **112.** The remaining one is of the colour of butter. **114.** By that are explained the silk and silk-cloth from the land of Chīna [China].

[COTTON, ORDINARY]

115. Cotton fabrics from Madhurā, the Aparāntas, the Kaliṅgas, Kāshī, the Vaṅgas, the Vatsas [capital: Kausambi] and the Mahīshas [Mahishmati on the Narmada] are the best.

Note: K.P. Kangle's translation in his *The Kautilya Arthaśāstra,* Part II, Delhi, 1986, pp. 103–05, occasionally modified, partly on the basis of his own annotation, and after comparison with his edited text, Part I, Delhi, 1986, pp. 54–55.

Extract 4.5
Cash Endowments at Interest: Two Inscriptions

A. Ushavadāta's Nasik Cave Inscription, Year 45 (c. AD 100)

Success! In the year 42, in the month Vesākha, Ushavadāta, son of

Dinika, son-in-law of king (*rāño*) Nahapāna, the K<u>sh</u>aharāta *K<u>sh</u>atrapa*, has bestowed this cave on the *Saṁgha* generally; he has also given a perpetual endowment (*ak<u>sh</u>aya-nivi*) of three thousand – 3000 – *kāhāpaṇas*, which, for the members of the *Saṁgha* of any sect and any origin dwelling in this cave, will serve as cloth money and money for extra robes [during rainy seson] (*kushaṇa-mūla*) and these *kāhāpaṇas* have been invested in guilds (*shreṇi*) dwelling at Govadhana, [of which] 2000 in a weavers' (*kolikanikaye*) (guild), interest (*v<u>ri</u>dhi*) one *paḍika* per hundred [monthly] and 1,000 in another weavers' (guild), interest (*vadhi*) three-quarters *paḍika* per cent; and those *kāhāpaṇas* are not to be repaid, their interest only to be enjoyed. Out of them the two thousand – 2000 – at one *paḍika* per cent, are the cloth money; out of these to every one of the twenty monks who keep the *vassa* in my cave a cloth money of twelve (*kāhāpaṇas*). As to the thousand which have been invested at an interest of three-quarters of a *paḍika* per cent, out of these the money (*mūla*) [is] for *kushāṇa*. And at the village of Chikhalapadra in the Kapura district (*ahāra*) have been given eight thousand – 8000 – stems of coconut trees; and all this has been proclaimed (*srāvita*) and registered (*nibadha*) at the town/mercantile assembly (*nigama-sabhā*) at the record office, according to custom.

Again, the donation made by the same in the year 41, on the fifteenth of the bright half of Kārttika, has in the year 45, on the fifteenth . . . been settled on the venerable gods and Brāhmaṇas, viz. seventy thousand – 70,000 – *kar<u>sh</u>āpaṇas* [so spelt here], each thirty-five making a *suvarṇa* (gold coin), a capital (therefore) of two thousand *suvarṇas*. (This is registered) at the record office according to custom.

Note: E. Senart's translation, *Epigraphia Indica*, VII, pp. 82–85, slightly modified, and incorporating a suggestion on the meaning of *kushaṇa-mūla* by E.J. Rapson. The word *nigama* in *nigama-sabhā* can mean both town and merchant, and even a company of merchants, as in the *Rāmāyaṇa*.

B. Mathura Inscription of the Reign of Huvi<u>sh</u>ka, Kushān year 28, c. AD 188

Success! In the year 28, on the first day of Gorpiaios, this eastern hall of merit (*puṇyashāla*) was given a perpetual endowment (*ak<u>sh</u>aya-nīvī*) by Kanasarukamāna's son, Kharāsalerapati, the *Vakanapati.* From what is cleared off, month by month (*mās-ānumasaṁ*) from the interest (*vriddhi*), therefrom hundred Brāhmaṇas should be served in the open hall, and day by day, having kept it at the entrance (*dvāra*) to the merit-hall (*puṇya-shālā*), on the same day, 3 *aḍhaka* pieces, one *prastha* (of) salt (*lavriṇa*), one *prastha shaku* (?), 3 jars (*ghaṭakas*) and 5 bowls (*mallaka*) of green vegetable bundles (*harita-kalāpaka*), this should be given for the destitute people, hungry and thirsty. And what merit (*puṇya*) is herein, may that accrue to the Devaputra Shāhi Huvishka, and also to those to whom the Devaputra is dear, and may this merit accrue to the whole earth (*prithivī*). The perpetual endowment (*akshaya-nivī*) was given to the – *rāka* (?) guild (*shreṇi*), 550 *purāṇas*, and to the flour-maker (*samitakara*) guild (*shreṇi*), 550 *purāṇas*.

Note: Sten Konow's translation, *Epigraphia Indica*, XXI, p. 60, modified.

Extract 4.6
Use of the Monsoons for Navigation: Two Classical Accounts

A. Pliny (d. AD 70): Natural History

In after times [i.e. subsequent to Alexander] it was considered safest for the voyage from Syagrus, the promontary (cape) in Arabia to Patale [at head of the Indus delta], to be performed by aid of a west wind, which is there called Hypalus, the distance reckoned to be 1,332 miles. The age that followed pointed out a shorter and safer route from the same cape to Sigerus [unidentified], a seaport of India, and for a long time this route was followed until one shorter was discovered by a merchant, and India was brought nearer us through love of gain. So, then, at the present day, voyages are made to India every year: and companies of archers are carried on board because the Indian seas are infested by pirates. And it will not be amiss to set out the whole of the voyage from Egypt, now that reliable knowledge of it is for the first time accessible. It is an important subject in view of the fact that in no year does India absorb less than fifty million sesterces [1 sesterce = ¼ denarius] of our [Roman] empire's wealth, sending back merchandise to be sold among us at a hundred times its prime cost. . . . It is advantageous to sail to India from Ocelis [Arabian port at the southern end of the Red Sea]. If the wind called Hippalus be blowing, Muziris [port in Kerala], the first mart of India, can be reached in forty days. . . . Travellers sail back from India in the beginning of the Egyptian month of Tybis – our December – or at all events before the 6th day of the Egyptian month Mechir, that is, before the Ides [the 13th] of January. In this way they can go and return the same year. They sail from India with a south-east wind, and on entering the Red Sea, catch the south-west or south.

Note: Translation of John W. McCrindle, *Ancient India as Described in Classical Literature*, London 1901 / Patna, 1987, pp. 111–12, but modified and extended by reference to studies in F. de Romanis and A. Tchernia (eds.), *Crossings: Early Mediterranean Contacts with India*, New Delhi, 2005.

B. The Anonymous Periplus of the Erythraean Sea (pre-AD 106)

57. The whole coastal route just described from Kané [Qani‘] and Eudaimon Arabia [Aden], men formerly used to sail over in smaller vessels, following the curves of the bays. The ship-captain Hippalus, by plotting the location of the ports of trade and the configuration of the sea, was the first to discover the route over open water. . . . In this region just as the winds we call ‘Etesian’ [north-western winds in the Mediterranean blowing for about forty days in summer] blow seasonally from the direction of the ocean, so a south-westerly wind makes its appearance in the Indian Sea, but it is called Hippalus after the name of the one who first discovered the way across. Because of this, right up to the present, some leave directly from Kané, and some from Aromata, and whoever are bound for Limyrike [*rect.* Dimyrike, Tamil Nadu] hold out with the wind on the quarter for most of the way, but whoever are bound for Barygaza [Bharuch] and whoever for Skythia [Sindh], [are thus retarded] for three days and no more, and, carried along the rest of the run on their own proper course, away from the shore on the high seas, over the [ocean] off the land, they bypass the aforementioned bays.

Note: Lionel Casson’s translation in his *The Periplus Maris Erythraei*, Princeton, 1989, pp. 86–87, slightly modified and with some bracketed explanations added.

Note 4.1

Elementary Concepts from Economics

While studying economic history one needs to be familiar with certain elementary terms and concepts used in Economics. **Economics** is usually defined as a science that studies relations among persons based on the processes of production, exchange, distribution and consumption of goods, and the rendering of services. *Goods* are things that are *produced* for consumption: thus books are goods, but rain-drops (being free gifts of nature) are not. *Services* are restricted to labour that is not spent in production or distribution of goods, but is directly applied to the satisfaction of human wants, such as that of personal servants, physicians or teachers. Since goods are limited in quantity and services are confined to human labour power, Economics is often called the science that deals with the use of 'scarce means'.

Goods produced for **exchange**, and not directly for consumption by the producer, are called *commodities*. Exchange consists of two forms: *barter*, where goods are directly exchanged for one another, and *sale,* where a good's possessor parts with it against payment received in money. *Money* is any set of goods (grain, gold, silver or copper pieces in very early times, or coins, currency notes, electronic accounts, etc., today) that serve as a medium of exchange and a measure of value. It is also the most 'liquid' or convertible form of storage of wealth. *Exchange value* (or, simply, 'value') is largely synonymous with price, but usually stands for approximate or long-term price of a good, rather than the actual market price at a particular moment.

A good carries an amount of money as its price or value, fixed by the pulls of *supply and demand*. Being scarce, the supply of a particular good will always be limited, while the capacity of consumers to pay for it (through the goods or money they possess) is also limited. Thus there will be a constantly shifting range within which the two pulls will set the price. As exchange transactions grow, a market is established. The *market* in Economics bears the special meaning of an area or zone in which competing sellers and buyers are so active and mobile (each looking for the best price from his point of view) that at any moment each good bears the same price in every part of the market. *Competition* ensures that any increase in demand and the resulting rise of price at one point will immediately attract suppliers from other parts, so that the price will rise everywhere as a result. Similarly, if supply increases at one point and prices fall there, buyers will rush from other parts to buy there, so that the demand, lessening at other places, prices will fall there as well. If there is no external constraint imposed on supply and demand, either by the state or by a *monopoly* firm, 'perfect competition' is said to prevail.

The theory of *marginal utility* seeks to explain what lies behind the pulls of supply and demand. It asks us to imagine all commodities as divisible into infinite units. With a definite amount of money to spend, each consumer will buy the commodities he wishes to consume, whose utility for him would decline as he proceeds with the consumption of further units of each. The utility of the last units of all commodities he buys with the last units of his money would have the same utility ('marginal utility') for him. On the other side, the producers would go on selling, with the unit costs rising, until the last units sold have the same *marginal cost*. This happens because of the increasing 'disutility' or 'pain' to the wage-earner over each additional dose of labour, and the growing aversion of the capitalist to the investment out of his resources of each additional unit of capital. The price and quantity of goods actually sold are, therefore, fixed at the point at which the demand curve, based on marginal utilities, and the supply curve, based on marginal costs, intersect.

There is no doubt that the marginal utility theory is an ingenious way of explaining the relationship between use value (utility) and exchange value (price) that classical (pre-1870) Economics was unable to do. But it hardly resolves the basic question, what creates exchange value? This is because, if we look at the matter closely, we find that the consumer's sense of utility must depend on his income. Thus marginal utilities themselves are determined by the wages and other earnings of the consumers that constitute the sum of all individual incomes in an economy. But, as we have just seen, these earnings themselves constitute the costs that are paid for by the amounts consumers pay. We are thus placed in a circular situation, where the basic factor that creates income itself eludes us.

A better way of understanding the problem is possible if we were to begin again and to imagine an exchange of goods taking place between two parties, each of whom is both a consumer and producer at the same time. Let us suppose that there is a jungle of some size with two persons in it. One (A) has collected fruits, the other (B) has killed an animal. They meet to exchange fruit for meat. A would be willing to part, at the maximum, with as much fruit the labour of collecting which is equal, for him, to the labour of hunting for a particular amount of meat by himself. Conversely, the maximum amount of meat B would part with would be determined by the labour necessary for him to collect the amount of fruit he wished to have, which equals the labour spent on the meat that he is parting with. An exchange will take place only if what each has to part with is less than the maximum quantity he had thought he could give away to escape the labour he would himself need to spend on getting the other good. We thus see that the utility (or costs) on both sides will be set by their expectations of labour to be spent by them if they went out to get the other good themselves. In essence, then, we have come to the classical economists' **labour theory of value**, where value is presumed to be determined by the amount of labour that the product embodies.

In a complex economy, it is true, the situation is not as simple. Even in the case we have considered, there are three *factors of production*. One is *land*, which, to economists, means all natural resources, including mineral wealth, agricultural land and (as in the case just considered) forest. Secondly, there is *labour*. Thirdly, *capital*, which in our primitive case would include the basket to carry fruit, and the bow and arrow by which to shoot down wild animals. With the passage of time, the forms which capital takes become more and more diverse and numerous, and include ploughs, cattle, artisans' tools, buildings and machinery, as well as stocks of goods and money. The owners of land and capital, once they become articles of private property, lay claims to shares in the value of goods, through extracting rent for the use of land, and interest and profit for the use of capital. Since these exactions have to be paid out of the price in almost every product, the price cannot be restricted to costs of labour (including costs of replacement or 'depreciation' of physical capital previously made by labour). How, then, can value be determined any longer by the quantum of labour spent on the product?

Karl Marx resolved this puzzle by showing that while the value of a good is indeed determined by the amount of labour that has gone into producing it, the cost of that labour itself (reflected in wages) is determined by the cost of subsistence of the labourer and his family, to the extent that this is necessary for the reproduction of the worker's *labour power*. But the labour expended in production of subsistence goods that he and his family consume is far less than the labour that he himself puts in as an employed worker. Thus human labour spent in a factory consists of two parts: labour necessary to buy enough goods to reproduce the labourer's subsistence, and *surplus labour* that creates *surplus value,* i.e. value above wage-costs. The price of a good (its 'value'), therefore, consists of not only wage-costs, but also of surplus value, out of which profits, rents, etc., are paid. This difference between costs of labour and the value of product of labour can be easily seen in an example derived from agriculture. A peasant grows crops, out of which he maintains himself and his family at a bare level of subsistence, and pays a large amount of rent to the landlord. Such rent comes out of his *surplus labour*, that creates *surplus produce*. The only difference with the factory is that in the factory the capitalist employs workers to work for him and sells the product himself, whereas in the case of the peasant, the rent is paid out of a part of the peasant's produce which he himself sells on the market.

The *classes* of society which, by performing **labour,** create surplus for others, are defined in various ways according to their 'forms of labour'. In early societies, *slaves* were persons under the complete control of their master, who could put them to work in any manner he chose or even sell them. The term *serf* is applied to peasants who could not leave their land and had to go on paying rent and/or perform labour services for the lord or landlord. In modern industrial economies, peasants and labourers tend to be free persons in law (if not sometimes by social custom). At the same time, the various labouring classes are being reduced to a large class of **workers** who are employed by capitalists on wages, whether in factory or farm, and have no control over the disposal of what they produce. 'Proletariat' ('the propertyless') is another name for this class; and the term *proletarianization* is used for the economic processes whereby other categories of labourers, peasants, artisans, etc., turn into semi-industrial or industrial workers.

An important role in improving the productivity of labour has been played by the process called **division of labour**, whose significance Adam Smith greatly emphasized in his *Wealth of Nations* (1776). In the pre-machine age, the development of special skills not only increased productivity per head, but also helped to diversify products. Such division of labour, however, hindered the *mobility* of labour across professions, since learning new skills to enter a new occupation became increasingly difficult. In modern times, the introduction of machinery has done away with many specialized manual skills and so ensured a far greater degree of mobility of labour, through reducing it to an unspecialized form.

We can now turn to the two factors of production besides labour, viz. land and capital. While in classical Economics **land** was viewed as comprising resources freely bestowed by nature (see above), in actual fact, it is in present times mostly owned by individuals – a result achieved largely by force during different periods of the past. This puts a price on land, thereby enabling the *landlords* or land-owners to lease it out on *rent* to peasants. That rent may be in kind (i.e. a share of the crop or a particular amount of grain, etc.) or in the form of money. In the latter case, the system is given the designation of *cash nexus*.

Strict textbook definitions, as we have seen, would apply the word **capital** to even workmen's own tools. In ordinary usage, it simply means money employed in business; or, as some economists would put it, money or physical assets so employed as to produce an income. When money is lent out at interest, it is *usury capital*, or what in modern times is called 'banking capital'. When money is used to buy goods so as to sell these at profit, it represents *merchant capital*. When money is used to employ labour to produce, with assets such as land, buildings, tools and machinery owned by a *capitalist* (individual or firm), it is termed *industrial capital*. This is the usual form of capital in a modern capitalist economy. In pre-industrial economies, on the other hand, merchant capital often predominated.

We have so far not taken **services** into consideration. In a society where there is a free labour market, i.e. there is no slavery or other forms of bondage, the recompense for any service – or its value – should correspond to the quantity and quality (i.e. skill) of the labour undertaken, subject to the same factors of supply and demand as operate in the case of prices of goods. Unskilled labour generally tends to be undervalued because of the large source of supply available, while the work of highly trained and skilled purveyors of services is overvalued because of the small number of persons that seem able to obtain the requisite qualifications.

Development is deemed to occur only when there is an increase in per-capita income of a country. Per-capita income is obtained by dividing the Gross Domestic Product (GDP) or *National Income* by the numerical size of the population. On this theme, the reader is invited to consult Note 1.1 in the volume on *Indian Economy, 1858–1914*, in this series. Since the data that enable us to estimate the amounts of GDP and population for successive years in modern times are largely unavailable for earlier times, it is, perhaps, best to avoid the use of the word 'development' in the context of ancient or medieval economies.

A country does not only have trade within it, but also has **trade** with other countries. The total amount of a country's exports and imports of merchandise, valued in money, is called its *volume of trade*. Its *balance of trade* is represented by the relative values of exports and imports. If the exports carry greater value than imports, its balance of trade is said to be 'favourable'. But the balance of trade is not the same thing as the *balance of payments*. If country A exports, in value, more to country B than what it imports from it, and so has, let us say, a favourable balance of trade of Rs 50 crore, it may yet have an unfavourable balance of payments over the same period. This may come about if, for example, the capitalists of country B have invested large amounts of capital in country A, on which the latter has to pay them Rs 75 crore in interest and profits. We can immediately see that, despite a favourable balance of trade of Rs 50 crore, country A would have an unfavourable balance of payments amounting to Rs 25 crore, which must be paid either by further exports or by transferring gold or units of international money (like US Dollars or Euros today) to country B. India under colonial rule had a constantly favourable balance of trade, but always an unfavourable balance of payments, owing to the 'tribute' it was called upon to pay to Britain. Such tribute mainly consisted of direct transfers of tax revenues to Britain and profits from assets cheaply acquired (e.g. plantations) by Europeans in India.

Note 4.2
Bibliographical Note

There is no single book exclusively devoted to the economic history of the period. There are many valuable insights, though, in D.D. Kosambi, *Introduction to the Study of Indian History*, Bombay, 1956, Chapter VIII ('Interlude of Trade and Invasions'). Much useful information about economic life is contained in B.N. Mukherjee, *The Rise and Fall of the Kushāṇa Empire,* Calcutta, 1988, pp. 351–86; and there is a sub-chapter on the economy of the period in Ranabir Chakravarti, *Trade and Traders in Early Indian Society*, New Delhi, 2002/2007, pp. 50–63 (notes, pp. 70–74). The economic geography of India, AD 1–300, is surveyed in Irfan Habib and Faiz Habib, *Atlas of Ancient Indian History*, New Delhi, 2012, Chapter 9 (linked to Map 9).

U.N. Ghoshal, in his *Contributions to the History of the Hindu Revenue System*, second edition, Calcutta, 1972, sets out an analysis of the material in the *Arthashāstra* and other texts which were possibly compiled in our period, on pp. 121–218, and, then, has a short chapter ('Scythian Period'), pp. 249–54, on the information that the inscriptions offer on revenue administration and land-grants. D.N. Jha, *Revenue System in Post-Maurya and Gupta Times,* Calcutta, 1967, offers a critical and systematic treatment, but does not separately deal with our period. R.S. Sharma's *Sūdras in Ancient India*, Delhi, 1958, Chapter VI, has much information to offer on the conditions of the lower classes during the period 200 BC – AD 200 mainly drawn from legal, religious and literary texts.

John Marshall, *Taxila, An Illustrated Account of Archaeological Excavations*, 3 vols, Cambridge, 1951, is still the best, comprehensive account of any historical city excavated in this sub-continent. Ahmad Hasan Dani, *The Historic City of Taxila*, Paris, 1986, is a competent summary that also takes into account some later work at the site.

On guilds, R.C. Majumdar's pioneer work, *Corporate Life in Ancient India*, first edition, 1918, may be read in the third edition, revised by the author, Calcutta, 1969, where the evidence for guilds in our period is presented on pp. 29–36. On the monetary system, see S.K. Maity, *Early Indian Coins and Currency System,* New Delhhi, 1970. The major catalogues of coins of the Greek rulers, their successors and the Kushān emperors have already been mentioned in *Note 3.2*; to these may be added Edward James Rapson, *Catalogue of the Coins of the Andhra Dynasty, the Western Kṣatrapas, the Traikūṭaka Dynasty and the 'Bodhi' Dynasty* in the British Museum, London, 1908/1967.

E.H. Warmington, *The Commerce between the Roman Empire and India*, second edition, London, 1974 (with text of 1928 edition and an Appendix containing new data), is still the single major work on the theme of its title. Lionel Casson's *The Periplus Maris Erythraei: Text, with Introduction, Translation and Commentary*, Princeton, 1989, is indispensable for any study of this remarkable Greek commercial memoir. Among further contributions to the study of Indo-Roman relations may be mentioned Rosa Maria Cimino (ed.), *Ancient Rome and India*, New Delhi, 1994, and F. De Romanis and A. Tchernia (eds.), *Crossings: Early Mediterranean Contacts with India*, New Delhi, 1997/2005. Xinru Liu, *Ancient India and Ancient China: Trade and Religious Exchanges, AD 1–600,* New Delhi, 1994, deals in part with India's trade with China during our period. On India's contacts with South-east Asia and the history of Indian principalities and culture in that region, R.C. Majumdar's *Hindu Colonies in the Far East*, Calcutta, 1944, was the standard work when it was published; it naturally lacks the information gained from much archaeological work that has taken place after its appearance.

Note 4.1 is largely inspired by a chapter by Maurice Dobb, 'An Introduction to Economics', in William Rose (ed.), *An Outline of Modern Knowledge*, London, 1931, pp. 593–624. Those who do not have access to it may read Maurice Dobb's *Political Economy and Capitalism*, second edition, London, 1940/1953. Current textbook Economics may be studied in books like William Samuelson, *Economics*, eleventh edition, New Delhi, 1982 (also subsequent editions/reprints).

Index